Castle Ts

Edinburgh *and* the Lothians

Graham S. Coe

COECAST
Tavistock

Castle Touring Guides
Edinburgh and the Lothians

First Published 2006
© Graham S. Coe 2006

Published by COECAST, Tavistock

Available through GOBLINSHEAD
130B Inveresk Road, Musselburgh , EH21 7AY, Scotland
Tel: 0131 665 2894   Fax: 0131 653 6566   Email: goblinshead@sol.co.uk

British Library Cataloguing in Publication Data
A catalogue record for this book is available from the British Library.

ISBN 1 899874 37 2

Castle Touring Guides

THE EAST NEUK OF FIFE
Published in October 1995 and covered the castles of St Andrews, Randerston, Balcomie, Crail, Airdrie, Isle of May, Pittarthie, Kellie, Newark, Ardross, Kilconquhar, Largo, Pitcruvie, Lundin, Aithernie, Struthers and Scotstarvit.

THE HOWE OF FIFE
Published in 1996 and covered the castles of Carslogie, Kilmaron, Lordscairnie, Parbroath, Collairnie, Fernie, Monimail, Denmylne, Ballinbreich, Creich, Mountquhanie, Naughton, Easter Kinnear, Kirkton, Earlshall, Cruivie, Pitcullo and Dairsie.

THE HEART AND WEST OF FIFE
Published in 1999 and covered the castles of Falkland, Pitillock, Bandon, Leslie, Balgonie, Balfour, Maiden, MacDuff, Wemyss, West Wemyss, Ravenscraig, Seafield, Grange, Inchkeith, Pitteadie, Balwearie, Hallyards, Carden, Lochore, Strathendry, Corston, Myres, Aberdour, Couston, Otterston, Fordell, Inchcolm, Rosyth, Pittreavie, Dunfermline, Canmore, Pittencrieff, Abbot, Hill, Pitfirrane, Culross, Dunimarle, Tulliallan, Bordie, Killernie, Knockdavie, Balmuto and Rossend.

Other Scheduled Guides ...
BORDER REIVERS – six guides covering the marches on both sides of the border. Scheduled for April 2006 onwards.

Contents

About the Author

I have always had a general interest in castles, but until 1990 it was directed towards the significant buildings in the care of the national conservation bodies.

While on holiday that year, I bought Mike Salter's "Discovering Scottish Castles", which listed over 1000 castles regardless of structural state.

A touring holiday the following year started the lengthy objective of photographing all of them. For every well known / well-visited castle there seemed to be 20 others which were passed on a daily basis without anyone recognising their existence. Each of them concealed centuries of history.

Having been a devotee of Scottish holidays since 1981, it seemed natural to combine the two passions. What started as a hobby quickly developed into an opportunity to promote all castles and also raise the profile of other tourist attractions.

At the launch of my first guide at Fernie Castle, I overheard the Laird of Balgonie and Eddergoll trying to encourage fellow castle owners to form an organisation - but none of them had the time. I wrote to the Laird offering help, and subsequently conducted a mail-shot to all "occupied" properties. Some 70 responded, but not all of them positively. Nevertheless an inaugural meeting did take place at Culcreuch Castle in June 1996. (More details of the Scottish Castles Association can be found on pages 213-214).

I was born in Rotherham, educated at Maltby Grammar School and spent the first 23 years of my working life at British Steel. Starting as a Commercial Apprentice, my first attachment was in the Statistics Department. I then moved to the Hollerith Section, which was an early computer installation. There was an opportunity to go on a programming course (1963), and the rest as they say is history. My British Steel career was always centred in the Rotherham area, and it covered all of the technical and management roles. In 1984 the family (wife Janet and three children Paul, Neil and Michael) moved close to York, buying a village Post Office and Corner Shop. I changed career direction, into Local Government, but remained in the computer field.

Progression took me from Selby District Council to Boothferry Borough Council (Goole) and then to Stockton-on-Tees Borough Council, where I was appointed as Information Technology Manager in 1991. Having taken the Council through the Local Government Review of 1996, when Stockton became a unitary authority delivering all local services, I then joined Ultracomp Ltd as a Principal Consultant covering all Information Technology and Local Government issues. In 2002 I moved to Meritec Ltd in a similar capacity.

In my leisure time overseas holidays are very important to me having visited Australia, Singapore, Hong Kong, Egypt, South Africa, Fiji, New Zealand, America and Sri Lanka, which have also re-kindled my interest in bird watching. During the winter nights the focus turns to running a quiz league.

Returning to my interest in castles, I have now photographed over 800 in Scotland, 300 plus in England and many in Wales and Ireland, not forgetting a few in Belgium, Germany, Spain and the Netherlands. Taking a short break in Normandy I was drawn to visiting the chateaux, which very quickly progressed into the basis for another series of guidebooks scheduled for future years.

It is the intention of this guide and all future guides to be accurate in all respects. If you find any mistakes, inaccuracies, oversights or additional material worthy of inclusion, then it will help future publications. Send your suggestions to Mr G S Coe - email grahamscoe@yahoo.co.uk.

Edinburgh *and* the Lothians

Acknowlegements

It is impossible to pay tribute to everyone who has supported the production of this guidebook, but here is an attempt to recognise the major contributors. Since 1997 I have been indebted to the help, advice, guidance and most importantly the friendship of John Pringle whose knowledge of fortified buildings, its history, structure and location is second to none. In particular in this part of Scotland we have spent many enjoyable hours roaming the countryside in search of the fortified buildings, which at times have been minimal. He has been a photographer for more than fifty years, starting at the age of ten with a Baby Brownie, and passed through the RAF School of Photography during his national service. Following retirement from a career in international finance, he has worked as a freelance photographer, specialising in mountains and in all subjects relating to Scotland's history. He is regular contributor to Muirhead calendar.

Since meeting Martin Coventry in 1997, he has been the inspiration primarily through his "The Castles of Scotland", which has become the de facto standard for all castle enthusiasts. He manages the design through to distribution of the guidebook.

As always The Royal Commission on the Ancient and Historical Monuments of Scotland (RCAHMS) have been very supportive, especially Geoffrey Stell, Veronica Fraser and Kristina Watson. The Commission's Inventory has been the major source for the background to all the structures, and to recognise that fact, entries in the guidebook have been marked with an ★.

The response for information and/or support from castle owners was immeasurable, and therefore thanks go to the following: - D.A Walker Business Consultants (Alderstone House), John D McCulloch (Auchindinny), M R A Matthews (Cruden Investments Ltd), Balgone House, the Earl of Rosebery (Barnbougle Castle), Robert Douglas Miller (Bavelaw Castle), Charles Spence (Biel), Brunstane House, Sir Robert M Clerk Bt. (Brunstane Castle), Alex Wallace – Headmaster (Bruntsfield House), Michael Bennett-Levy (Carberry Tower), Andrew Hunter – Headmaster Merchiston Castle School (Colinton Castle), Ludovic Broun-Lindsay (Colstoun House), Eric and Rona Jamieson (Cramond Tower), Sir Jack Stewart-Clark (Dundas Castle), Sally and Guy Turner (Elphinstone Tower), Ian and Sue Brash (Fa'side Castle), William R A Buchanan (Harlawhill), Ann Yuille – General Manager (Houstoun House), Alex Brownlee (Illieston House), Robin Barnes – City of Edinburgh Council (Lauriston Castle), Gordon Scott Thomson – Sales & Marketing Manager (Lennoxlove Castle), Nicholas Groves-Raines (Liberton House), Gordon Casely (Mannerston), CKD Galbraith (Mayshiel), Lord and Lady Elliott (Morton House), Janet Russell (Murieston Castle), Ann Southwood – Principal (Newbattle), Bill Cowan (Newton), Richard and Malin Nairn (Niddry Castle), Findlay M Lockie (Northfield House), Fr Donald – Guest master (Nunraw Castle), Hazel and John Hunter O.B.E (Ochiltree Castle), Prof. Juliet Cheetham (Peffermill House), John MacDonald – Bursar (Pinkie House, Thomas H Hardie (Prestongrange), Donald I Noble – Factor (Staneyhill Tower), Ian Simpson (Sydserf), Donald Vass – Factor (Tyninghame House), John R Findlay (West Port House), Andrew Murray (The Whitehouse), A.M Brander (Whittinghame Tower) and Francis G A Ogilvy (Winton).

Significant houses have been included, and I am indebted to Henrietta Dundas-Beeker (Arniston House) and William Hay (Melville Castle).

Thanks also to Philip's and Khol Dieu for the permission to use the maps.

Introduction

This guidebook covers the geographical (i.e pre 1975) areas of Edinburgh and the Lothians, although for ease of constructing circular tours, some of the sites have been "moved" between the areas e.g Newton (Midlothian) appears in one of the East Lothian tours.

To create manageable tours, the whole area has been divided into five sections — Edinburgh, East Lothian (east), East Lothian (west), Midlothian and West Lothian, to give a balanced spread of the 152 structures

It is believed that this book is the first to publish in the same volume a photograph of every fortified building with visible remains. Newhall, Kirkhill House, Beanston and Bonnington House have been excluded from the publication, until it has been demonstrated that they still contain fortified remnants.

On the other hand, because of their architectural significance some grand houses have been included at the end of the book in the Additional Information section: Hopetoun House, Arniston House, Dalmeny House, Melville Castle, Newliston and Newhailes.

From the vibrant streets of the capital city to wide, open seascapes and wild, rugged hills, Edinburgh and the Lothians captures the essence of Scotland. When you explore the area you follow the footsteps of kings and queens, none more so than in its built history.

In each of the sections there are structures to admire. In Edinburgh there is the much-visited Edinburgh Castle, Holyrood Palace and Craigmillar Castle, but has in its boundaries some fabulous buildings like Craigcrook Castle, Liberton House, Liberton Tower, Cramond Tower, Castle Gogar and Peffermill House. East Lothian boasts the awesome position of the ruins of Tantallon Castle, and the magnificent Dirleton Castle to the beautiful restorations of Ballencrieff House, Fa'side Castle and Fenton Tower, while not forgetting the home of the Duke of Hamilton's home Lennoxlove. Midlothian offers the eye-catching Crichton Castle, while giving the opportunity to stay at the impressive hotels of Borthwick and Dalhousie Castles. In West Lothian there is no shortage of variety of fortified buildings with the palace at Linlithgow; the stunning Blackness Castle guarding the Firth of Forth to the proud towers of Niddry Castle and Ochiltree Castle.

All in all there is much to admire outside of the popular attractions, and enjoy the Scottish capacity for hospitality and friendliness.

While some of the castles in the guide are open to the public and therefore details of access arrangements are included, the majority are on private land and can only be seen from a distance. Under no circumstances should they be visited without obtaining permission from the owners/occupiers.

Many castles are in a dangerous state and visitors should take extreme care before entering the building, even having sought the owners' permission.

How to Use This Guide

Please read the guide thoroughly, so that before you move on to the next castle, spend time exploring the towns and villages before moving on. There is a little detail of some of the towns in the guide.

The route is always circular (clockwise), which means that you can join it at any point and make a complete tour round if you wish. At the point of entry look at the next castle number (clockwise), refer to the appropriate page in the guide and the directions to that castle are usually at the bottom of the page.

Other places of interest en route are linked to the annexes within the "directions" instructions. To help the weary traveller overcome the frustration of not knowing where to stop for refreshments there is, occasionally reference to an inn, public houses or restaurants en route.

Fuller information should be sought from Tourist Information Centres, details of which are included in the guide.

Please check opening times of any tourist attraction, especially out of season. They do vary.

Do not forget your camera, a pair of binoculars, and Ordnance Survey Maps (Nos 65, 66 and 67).

Having said all that do not miss the scenery.

Castle Touring Guides

Edinburgh

Map 1 – Edinburgh

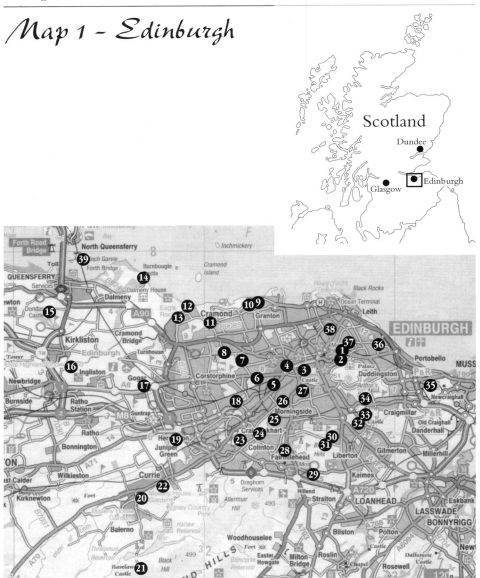

© Philip's 2003, © Crown copyright 2003

1 Croft-an-Righ House (*)

Ordnance Survey (OSR) = NT 271742

Start at Holyroodhouse car park, in Holyrood Park. Leave the car park and walk along the footpath by the east wall of the grounds of Holyroodhouse to Croft-an-Righ, a narrow lane; the House, occupied as offices, is a few yards along on the left.

Structure

It is L-shaped on plan with the re-entrant angle facing south. The main block contained three storeys and the wing four. The top floor of the former being lower than that of the latter, it was originally lit by dormers; but the wall-heads have been raised throughout, those of the wing sufficiently to include an additional storey, which was lit by dormers. The masonry was rubble, once harled, with chamfered and rounded dressings. Turrets and conical roofs projected from the south corners, and all three have been heightened and re-roofed.

Brief History

The house is popularly associated with the Regent Moray, Queen Mary's half-brother, who was assassinated at Linlithgow on January 23rd 1569-70, a date which seems too early for any part of the present fabric. Sir Daniel Wilson has pointed out that it answers generally to the description of a house, sometime the property of Lord Elphinstone, which William Graham, Earl of Airth, bought from the Earl of Linlithgow.

No access, visible from the lane.

Croft-an-Righ House

3

2 Holyroodhouse

Ordnance Survey (OSR) = NT 269739

Retrace your steps to the car park, and continue on foot past the Palace gates and along Abbey Strand to the entrance.

Structure

The earliest part of the palace, circa 1528, is the south west corner of the church, with a circular turret at each angle, is the tower at the north-western corner of the palace.

Brief History

It originated as an abbey, founded in 1128, in the time of David I, but gave way to the building of the present palace, some parts of which were totally demolished by the English in 1543.

The members of the royal family often lodged here; parliaments of Robert Bruce and Edward Balliol were held in it; James I and his queen loved it; James II was born and crowned here; James III resided in it for lengthy periods; while James IV and subsequent kings identified it with the crown.

David Rizzio, Mary, Queen of Scot's secretary, was murdered here in her presence, and Bonnie Prince Charlie stayed here for six weeks in 1745.

The palace is the official residence of the monarch in Scotland.

The guide book available at the palace gives a full and detailed account of the building.

Open all year. Telephone 0131 556 1096 or web www.royal.gov.uk. Admission price.

Holyroodhouse

3 Edinburgh Castle

Ordnance Survey (OSR) = NT 252735

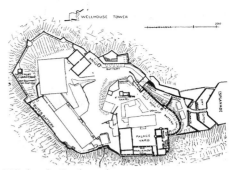

Edinburgh Castle – plan

Return to car park and drive past the entrance to the Palace to the mini roundabout at the foot of the Royal Mile; turn left into Canongate and continue up the hill past High Kirk of St Giles on left, to another mini roundabout at the top of Lawnmarket. Bear half left into Johnston Terrace and continue downhill until first available meter parking space. Near the top of the north side of Johnston Terrace there is a long flight of steps leading to the esplanade of Edinburgh Castle.

Structure

The northern, western and southern sides of the castle are precipitous and sometimes almost perpendicular. On some parts of the shoulders and the slopes, beyond the present ramparts are vestiges of former fortifications. On the north face stood a fragment called Wallace's Cradle, and at the base of that precipice was a small old ruin from 1450, called Wallace's Tower, in both cases being a corruption of Well-house.

Brief History

It is supposed to have been occupied as a military stronghold long before the Christian era. The Caledonian Reguli held it in the 5th century; they and the Northumbrian Saxons often sharply contested for the possession of it from 452 till the time of Malcolm II; and the Northumbrian king

Edwin reconstructed its fortifications about 626, and gave it the name of Edwinesburgh, afterwards transmuted into Edinburgh. It changed hands several times during the Wars of Independence, and was besieged and captured by the Douglases after the 6th Earl of Douglas was summarily executed at the Black Dinner in the castle in 1440. Mary of Guise died here and Queen Mary gave birth to James VI in 1566.

The castle is home to the Scottish Crown Jewels, the Stone of Destiny, the monstrous cannon Mons Meg and the Scottish National War Memorial.

Open all year. Telephone 0131 225 9846. In the care of Historic Scotland. Admission price.

Edinburgh Castle

4 East Coates House (*)

Ordnance Survey (OSR) = NT 241734

Return to the car by the same route and drive down to the foot of Johnston Terrace, and then take first right turn into Castle Terrace. Continue to the T-junction (traffic lights) and turn right into Lothian Road, keeping to the left lane. At the junction with the west end of Princes Street, take the second left turn after Caledonian Hotel into Shandwick Place, then first right into Stafford Street. At the end of Stafford Street, turn left along Melville Street and continue to T-junction, parking either near the end of Melville Street or just after turning right into Manor Place. At the north side of St Mary's Episcopal Cathedral stands East Coates House; there is a public footpath between the house and the cathedral.

Structure

This L-shaped, 17th century house was built of rubble, harl-pointed and of two storeys and an attic. Its main block runs roughly north and south and had circular turrets, entered from the attic floor, corbelled out from the south angles. The wing, which projected west from the north end, was intended for a scale-and-platt stair with a chamber above, access to which and to the upper storey of the main block was obtained from an existing turret-stair set out on conoidal corbelling within the re-entrant angle. The turret-stair also had a series of stepped corbels higher up, and was developed to a rectangular plan near the top in order that the roof of the wing may sweep over it unbroken. The gables were crow-stepped.

Brief History

John Byres, born in 1569, purchased the East Coates property about 1610. Thereafter he held office as Bailie, Dean of Guild and Treasurer of Edinburgh. He married first Mary Barclay of Towie Barclay, who died in 1616. Within a few years he had married Agnes Smith, daughter of Robert Smith, merchant burgess. In 1629 he died, and his tombstone still exists in Greyfriars Churchyard.

The building is used as the Episcopal Church's Theological Institute, and therefore permission should be sought to view, although can be seen from the road.

East Coates House

5 Dalry House

Ordnance Survey (OSR) = NT 235728

Return to your car and drive north on Manor Place, then turn left into Chester Street; at the traffic lights at the T-junction, turn left into Palmerston Place and continue to the traffic lights at the junction with West Maitland Street, keeping to the right lane at the lights. Cross straight over to Torphichen Street and take the first right turn into Dewar Place, keeping to the left lane. Turn right again down Morrison Street, again keeping to the left lane. At the next traffic lights (left filter) at Haymarket junction, turn left along Dalry Road and take the fifth left turn into Orwell Place; Dalry House (council premises) is on the left.

Structure

The building dates from 1661, and has hexagonal stair-towers and fine plaster work. After being harled, whitewashed and renovated in 1965 it is now an old people's day centre.

Brief History

The house was said to be haunted by "Johnnie One Arm". John Chiesly was executed for shooting Sir George Lockhart of Carnwath, after Lockhart found against Chiesly in a divorce settlement. Chiesly had his arm chopped off before being hanged, but his dead body was taken from the gallows before he could be buried. In 1965 the remains of a one-armed man are said to have been found under a hearth.

Can be viewed from the road.

Dalry House

6 Roseburn House

Ordnance Survey (OSR) = NT 226731

Roseburn House

Return to Dalry Road and turn right, continuing back to the traffic lights at Haymarket junction, keeping to the left lane. Turn left along Haymarket Terrace and then West Coates until traffic lights at Roseburn Bar. Turn left into Roseburn Street and park just before gates to Murrayfield rugby stadium. Roseburn House is on the same side of the street as the rugby ground and the rear of the building can be seen from Roseburn Crescent, which runs parallel to, and to the north west of, Roseburn Street.

Structure

The original entrance was by the doorway in the north-west turret, which also contained a wheel-staircase. A scale and platt stair had been added on the east side in the 17th century, with a new entrance doorway, and an extension of the east front had been formed at the same time. The ground floor is vaulted, and although greatly altered, it had indications of carefully finished mason work.

Brief History

The earliest charter connected with Roseburn is dated 1697, when Sir James Scougal, Senator of the College of Justice, obtained a charter, under the Great Seal, of the lands, with the mills of Dalry, which were then and in all time coming ordained to be called the lands of Roseburn.

Private residence, but it is partially visible from the road.

Roseburn House

7 Ravelston House

Ordnance Survey (OSR) = NT 217741

Return along Roseburn Street to the Roseburn Bar junction and then turn left into Roseburn Terrace; continue along Corstorphine Road and turn right immediately after the Murrayfield Hotel, up Murrayfield Road. At the T-junction just after Murrayfield Golf Course clubhouse, turn left along Ravelston Dykes. On the right hand side, after a little more than 0.25 miles, stands the remaining stair tower of Ravelston House in the garden of a private house; do not attempt to turn right into narrow lane but continue and park near junction of Ravelston Dykes and Craigcrook Road. Return on foot to narrow lane and view stair tower over garden wall.

Structure

Within the gardens of Ravelston House are preserved some architectural details that survived the fire in which the original mansion was destroyed. From these it appears that the house was probably a Z-planned structure dating form the early 17th century. The remains comprise a range of outbuildings and a small rectangular tower, now free standing, which housed the turnpike and in which the entrance was situated. The masonry was of rubble and had been harled; the dressings at voids had the arrises rounded off at jamb and lintel. The entrance doorway was similarly treated, but a more elaborate doorway was subsequently placed within the opening.

Brief History

The pilaster friezes were initialed G.F and I.B for George Foulis, first of Ravelston, and Janet

Ravelston House

(Joneta) Bannatyne, his wife; the lintel was panelled and is inscribed "NE QVID NIMIS" (Moderation in all things) 1622. He was the second son of James Foulis of Collington and his lady, Anne Heriot.

In 1726 the property was sold to Alexander Keith.

In the garden of a private house, view from the road or request permission from the occupants.

8 Craigcrook Castle (*)

Ordnance Survey (OSR) = NT 211742

Return to car and turn left on to Craigcrook Road. After a little more than 0.25 miles Craigcrook Castle stands on the left, a little way back from the road.

Structure

The castle was built around 1545. Excluding modern extensions, the plan comprises a main block, to which two towers were attached. The northern tower, projecting from the north wall midway in its length, is rectangular, and was built to contain the staircase, while the other, projecting from the south-western angle, was a slightly tapering cylinder. Circled turrets to contain small turnpikes were corbelled out, one midway along the south wall, the other within the western re-entrant angle. Two other circled angle-turrets, one of which survives, graced the east gable.

It is a plain rubble built harled structure, consisting of a basement, two upper storeys and a garret. The gables were crow-stepped. The cylindrical tower contained a basement and three upper floors; it rose above the main roof and terminated in an open lookout paved with stone and enclosed within a relatively modern crenellated parapet of ashlar, resting on the original continuous corbelling of one member.

Brief History

The castle has been inhabited since the beginning of its existence, when it was a keep for the defence and provisioning of Edinburgh in the event of a siege.

The lands of Craigcrook have a longer history than the house, and according to a Deed of 1362 were held by a family called Graham, who gave the lands to John de Alyncrum, a burgess of Edinburgh. He settled

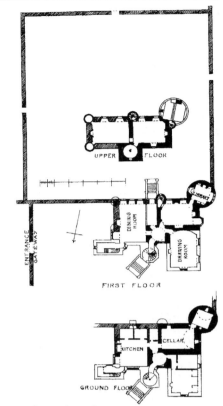

Craigcrook Castle – plans

the lands or the income from them on a Chaplaincy of St Giles. Somehow the situation changed, nearly 20 years before the Reformation of 1560, and the Provost of Edinburgh, Sir Simon Preston of Craigmillar made over the lands to Sir Edward Majoribanks, styled Prebend of Craigcrook. He let the lands for a year to George, brother of Sir James Kirkcaldy of Grange, who held Edinburgh Castle for Queen Mary until compelled to surrender it.

In 1542 the Prebend assigned the lands in feu farm to William Anderson, a burgess of Edinburgh and known as "Adamson of Craigcrook". He is believed to have been a son of Bailie Adamson, a Guardian of Edinburgh, after Flodden (1513). Bailie

Adamson was killed at the Battle of Pinkie in 1547. Adamson of Craigcrook built the castle and Walter Adamson added to the building in 1626 and about 1656 John Muir, merchant of Edinburgh, owned the castle and altered the surrounding wall.

Sir John Hall, Baronet of 1687, Lord Provost of Edinburgh became the next owner but sold it to Walter Pringle, who sold it to John Strachan, Clerk to the Signet. Strachan left the property for charitable purposes in 1719 and the trust still discharges the Testator's wishes with a widening scope. Archibald took over the lease in the early part of the 19th century. In 1815 it became the summer residence of Lord Jeffrey, Senator of the College of Justice, who occupied it till his death. Robert Croall of Edinburgh rented the property in 1874 when he and his family retained the tenancy until the death of Douglas Croall in 1966. It was restored from 1986.

The castle is occupied as offices for Scottish Field (www.scottishfield.co.uk). Please make a written request to view from the outside.

Craigcrook Castle

9 Caroline Park House (*)

Ordnance Survey (OSR) = NT 227773

Continue along Craigcrook Road and, at traffic lights, cross straight over Queensferry Road to Quality Street. At the mini roundabout turn right into Main Street and continue to offset T-junction with Silverknowes Road East; turn right and drive along Ferry Road for just over a mile until the large roundabout at Crewe Toll. Turn left down Crewe Road North for half a mile until junction with West Granton Road. Continue straight on at the junction down a narrow lane until its end is reached, with a small space for parking. To the right of the foot of the lane stands Caroline Park House; the late 17th century exterior can be seen from the gateway, but the late 16th century work is in the internal courtyard.

Structure

There were two entrances, and were centrally situated in the north and south wings. The northern was the principal, the main approach being from the north-east, where the fine entrance gate piers still remain. They are contemporary with the present south front of the house, which was embellished by Tarbat in 1696, and probably superseded the plainer entrance gate adjacent.

The house was a low-set harled structure of two storeys in all wings but that on the south, where upper chambers were contrived within the roofs. The lateral wings have coupled roofs received on skewed gables of eccentric form. The central portion had a flat roof surmounted by a good balustraded parapet with well-moulded stone balusters square on plan and diagonally disposed.

Brief History

The barony of Royston marched with the barony of Granton, and the respective mansions were adjacent. In 1740 when John, second Duke of Argyll and Greenwich, the then proprietor of Royston, purchased the

Caroline Park House

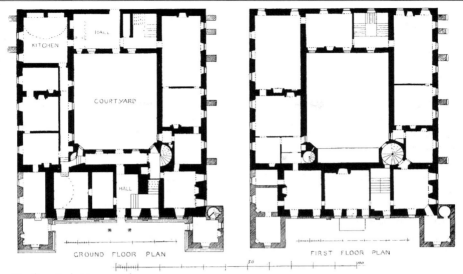

Caroline Park House – plans

Granton property he combined the two estates under the name of Caroline Park after his eldest child, who married the Earl of Dalkeith. The house has been continuously occupied since its erection in 1685 by Sir George Mackenzie, who in that year was created Viscount Tarbat and later Earl of Cromarty.

Occupied as offices, therefore please make a written request to view the exterior.

Caroline Park House

10 Granton Castle

Ordnance Survey (OSR) = NT 225772

Return to the car parking space and follow a footpath heading north beside a wall. After some distance, part of the corner of the old wall of Granton Castle is inset in the wall and also an old doocot for the castle; continue on the footpath and turn right at West Shore Road where the gate piers for the castle can be seen.

Structure

Originally it was an L–plan, but only the gates and some walling remain. The original part of the house was in the style prevalent in the 16th century, and it was probably built after the English invasion in 1544, when Hertford landed his troops at Granton.

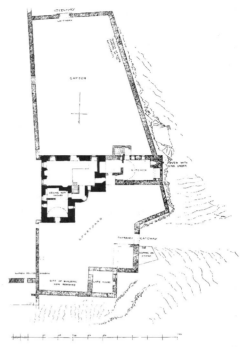

Granton Castle – plan

Granton Castle (c. 1890)

Brief History

The property of Easter Granton from 1479 to 1592 belonged to the Melvilles of Carnbee in Fife. After passing through the hands of several proprietors, Granton became the property, in 1619, of Sir Thomas Hope of Craighall, who during the reign of Charles I made it his principal residence. The house and property were bought in 1740 by the Duke of Argyll and Greenwich, and added to his estate of Caroline Park.

Granton Castle – gates and some walling (all that remains)

Site freely visible from the road.

11 Lauriston Castle (*)

Ordnance Survey (OSR) = NT 204762

After returning to the car, drive back along the lane and turn right into West Granton Road. Continue straight on through two roundabouts along Muirhouse Parkway, Silverknowes Parkway and Lauriston Farm Road until a T-junction with Cramond Road South. Turn right and then right again almost immediately into the grounds of Lauriston Castle; there is a car park just within the gates.

Structure

It is a large and mainly modern structure, which has grown around the late 16th century tower forming the south-west angle of the present mansion. The tower is a structure of three storeys and an attic, and is oblong in plan. It had on the north a central projecting tower, which was circled at base where it housed a turnpike, and rectangular above, where it contained bed chambers. The turnpike ascended only to the second floor; the chambers above it were reached by a small turret-stair corbelled out in the north-west re-entrant angle. Larger turrets, within which were chambers, were corbelled out at the southern angles above first floor level and rose to the wall-head; the sill of the upper turret-window looking west projected as a shelf for a lantern. The masonry is of rubble.

Brief History

Archibald Napier who had purchased the estate from the Forresters of Corstorphine around 1587 built it. In 1683 it was bought by William Law, goldsmith in Edinburgh and then passed on to his son, the famous financier, John Law (1671-1729). It became the residence of the Rt Hon Andrew Lord Rutherford (1791-1854) and then became the seat of Thomas MacKnight Crawfurd of Cartsburn.

Owned by the City of Edinburgh Council, the grounds are open during daylight hours, and the castle is open for guided tours – tel 0131 336 2060 or email lauriston.castle@tiscali.co.uk.

Lauriston Castle

12 Cramond Tower (*)

Ordnance Survey (OSR) = NT 191770

Return to the gates and turn right along Cramond Road South and follow the main road until the right turn into Cramond Glebe Road. Just before Cramond Inn turn right into the public car park behind the inn. The rear of Cramond Tower stands just to the south of the car park. To see the front of the tower, leave the car park and walk a little way back up Cramond Glebe Road, then turn left into Kirk Cramond; a little way beyond the excavated remains of the Roman fort, the tower can be seen through its gateway on the left.

Cramond Tower

Structure

The tower probably dates from the late 15th or early 16th century. It is, on plan, an oblong from north to south. From the southeast angle there projected a circled stair tower. Beneath the wall-head there were four storeys, of which the lowest and the uppermost were ceiled with barrel-vaults. The tower today is freestanding, but in the past there stood against the east wall a three-storeyed addition, while a four-storeyed extension was reared against the west wall; against the north wall there may have been a two-storeyed addition. The masonry of the tower was freestone rubble with dressed corners, and shell pinnings were extensively employed. The entrance is at ground level in the south wall at its junction with the stair-tower. The doorway has had a semicircular head, rebated, like the jambs, to accommodate outer and inner doors.

Brief History

The Bishops of Dunkeld possessed part of the lands of Bishops Cramond, in the time of William the Lion (1165-1214), and two bishops died here, the second bishop in 1173, and the seventh in 1214. Following its acquisition by Robert de Cardney, Bishop of Dunkeld, it was alienated by a successor, James Paton in 1574 to Archibald Douglas of Kilspindie, himself a descendant of Archibald (Bell the Cat), Earl of Angus. He in turn alienated it and the surrounding lands to Alexander Douglas, a macer in Edinburgh, who the sold the property in 1622 to James Inglis, a city merchant. One of Mr. Inglis's successors, Sir John Inglis of Cramond, was at one time Postmaster General of Scotland. Eric and Rona Jamieson acquired the tower in 1978, which had been empty for over two centuries, and began the restoration programme. It was completed in 1983.

It is a private property but it can be seen from the road. The owners are members of the Scottish Castles Association and contribute to its visiting programme, which may include from time to time Cramond Tower.

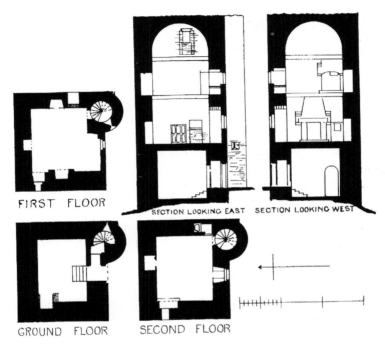

FIRST FLOOR

SECTION LOOKING EAST   SECTION LOOKING WEST

GROUND FLOOR   SECOND FLOOR

Cramond Tower – plans and sections

13 The Whitehouse

Ordnance Survey (OSR) = NT 187766

From the car park, drive back up Cramond Glebe Road and turn right at T-junction into Whitehouse Road. After approximately 0.75 miles The Whitehouse can be seen behind garden walls on the right (west) side.

Structure

It was a 16th-century L-plan tower house. When excavating a recess in the north wall of the dining room it was found to have been one of the original outside walls of the house, on which the whitewash and harling were found intact. The original doorway passing through this wall under a rough archway, with the iron frogs on which the door was hung, was found, having been, before the dining and drawing rooms were built, the main entrance to the house.

Brief History

The first reference to Whitehouse is found in the will of Gilbert Primrois, principal surgeon to James VI, who died at Westminster on 18th April 1616. David Primrose acquired Whyte House from John and James Logan in October 1615, and James, brother of David, held the estate until 1676 when he sold it to William Corse. Acquiring the property John Menzies sold it to his son-in-law, George Adie in 1719, and when he died in 1750 his son, David, who immediately sold it to David Strachan, a relative of John Strachan of Craigcrook, succeeded him. He died in 1771 but the sundial is still preserved which bears his initials and the date of 1752. Within two years his son and heir died, but he had conveyed the lands and estate to Trustees, and they conveyed the whole lands and house to Wilhelmina, Lady Glenorchy.

Founder of the Barnton family, William Ramsay, purchased the house in 1788 and they held it for some 80 years during which time many alterations were made.

Private residence: visible from the public highway.

The Whitehouse

14 Barnbougle Castle

Ordnance Survey (OSR) = NT 169785

Continue on Whitehouse Road until the junction with Queensferry Road, at Barnton Hotel. Turn right on to Queensferry Road and continue for approximately 2 miles to the slip road leading to B924, signposted South Queensferry. After approximately 0.5 miles, turn right into the Dalmeny House Estate. Use the car park for Dalmeny House and follow the footpath north to Barnbougle Castle, visible through trees by the shore. At other times of the year it is possible to reach Barnbougle Castle along the Shore Walk from Cramond (via ferry) to the east or South Queensferry to the west.

Structure

Barnbougle is situated on the seashore north of Dalmeny House. Prior to 1880 it was a shell, before it was entirely reconstructed according to the original plans, and, therefore only some original segments can be seen, principally from the shore.

Brief History

It belonged to the Moubrays in the 12th century, was sold in 1615 to Sir Thomas Hamilton, later Earl of Haddington, and was re-sold in 1662 to Sir Archibald Primrose, who became Lord Justice General of Scotland, and his younger son, the 1st Earl, and their successors lived in it until Dalmeny House was built about 1815. At some time subsequent there was an explosion in the cellars, which had been used to store gunpowder for the quarry. Most of the north-west wall and the rectangular tower in the north-east survived. In 1881 the 5th Earl of Rosebery rebuilt the castle using the existing cellars and remaining walls.

To view the exterior permission must be sought from Dalmeny House. Details of Dalmeny are on page 200.

Barnbougle Castle

15 Dundas Castle (*)

Ordnance Survey (OSR) = NT 116767

On leaving the estate, turn right on the B924 and drive under the Forth (railway) Bridge and through South Queensferry High Street, and then turn left on to the B907 (The Loan) before reaching the Forth Road Bridge. Drive straight on until a roundabout and then turn left on to B8000. After approximately half a mile there is a small road on the right leading into the Dundas Castle Estate (sign at entrance). The original tower stands close to the 19th-century Dundas Castle.

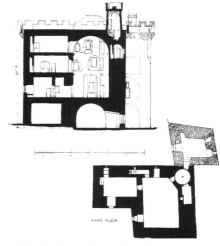

Dundas Castle – plan and section

Structure

Dundas is a 15th century L-shaped tower of four storeys. A second wing was added projecting from the north-west angle. In the original tower, a newel-stair led from the entrance in the re-entrant to the first floor.

The masonry is of rubble; the walls are surmounted by a continuous embattled parapet of the 16th century.

Brief History

The Dundas family held the estate from around 1124 till 1875 when the trustees of

Dundas Castle

James Russel purchased it. The tower was probably erected about 1416 under a warrant from Robert, Duke of Albany. In 1818 William Burn built a castellated Tudor-gothic mansion beside the tower, and it is now the stately home of Sir Jack Stewart-Clark and his wife, Lady Lydia.

Although the estate is privately owned and viewing of the tower is by appointment only, the castle is available for exclusive hire for weddings or corporate hospitality. Contact the General Manager on 0131 319 2039, email sales@dundascastle.co.uk or visit the web site at www.dundascastle.co.uk.

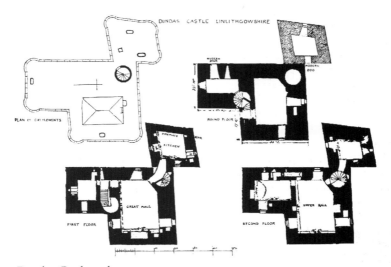

Dundas Castle – plans

21

16 Hallyards

Ordnance Survey (OSR) = NT 129738

From Dundas Castle turn left on the A8000 towards the bridge. At the two roundabouts go straight across, and continue on the B800 through Kirkliston. Straight ahead at the traffic lights. After 0.5 miles turn left on to the unclassified road; turn left at the t-junction and right at the junction with the farm buildings, and continue to an area for parking on the right hand side of the road. The few remains are in a small wooded area.

Hallyards – c. 1890

Structure

It was a mid 17th-century mansion built of rubble with freestone dressings and was oblong on plan. Below the wallhead were four storeys, while a garret was contained within the roof. A circular stair-tower was set in the east wall with an internal as well as an external projection. Over recent years continuous destruction has left it as a site scattered with stone.

Brief History

In 1619 there was a grant to John, Earl of Mar, of the lands of Halyairdis in the barony of Listoun. In 1630 the same lands with the manor were conferred by a charter on Mr John Skene, a clerk of the College of Justice.

It is on open land close to the runway of Edinburgh airport.

Hallyards – today

17 Castle Gogar (*)

Ordnance Survey (OSR) = NT 164730

Return through the farm buildings, and at next junction bear left and continue under the railway bridge to the junction with the A8. Turn left and travel for 2.5 miles to a large roundabout (keep in the left hand lane to the roundabout – signposted City Centre). Straight across and take the next left turn before the traffic lights, signposted Freight Terminal. After approximately 1 mile, close to the Turnhouse Golf Club clubhouse, Castle Gogar can be seen on the left on the far side of one of the airport runways.

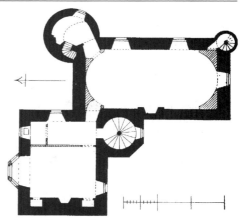

Castle Gogar – plan

Structure

It was built on a plan, which was analogous to the L-type, but diverged from it in minor details. The lateral wall of the wing was not a prolongation of a gable of the main block; instead, wing and main block were attached only at one corner. There were therefore two main re-entrant angles instead of the usual one, and windows were obtained in the gables of the wings. A second divergence from type was the cylindrical tower at the north-east angle of the main block, balancing a semi-octagonal tower in the south re-entrant angle. The south-east and south-west angles of the main block, and the north-west angle of wing, were graced with cylindrical angle-turrets borne on multi-membered continuous corbelling.

The house is four storeys and a garret in height; the walls were of rubble and were

Castle Gogar

rough-cast. The windows had back-set margins, chamfered at jamb and lintel. The gables are crow-stepped.

The tower was circled internally but above wall-head level was developed externally to a square by means of an angle corbelling, French rather than Scottish in detail.

Brief History
Adam Cowper, one of the Clerks of Session, whose title was ratified in 1601, purchased the lands of Gogar in the 16th century from Robert Logan of Restalrig, to whom they belonged. His son John, whose initials, with those of his wife, are carved, in various places on the building, built the house.

Private residence. Please make a written request for an external viewing.

18 Stenhouse (*)

Ordnance Survey (OSR) = NT 215717

Return to the junction at Maybury Casino and turn right and then left on to the A8 Glasgow Road, signposted Edinburgh city centre. After 0.75 miles turn right into Meadow Place Road, then left at the traffic lights (opposite entrance to Tesco) into Ladywell Road; continue along Corstorphine High Street and follow main road around bend to right into Saughton Road; take the first turning on the right into Dovecot Road where the doocot for Corstorphine Castle stands a little way along on the right. (The site of the castle is in the gardens of one of the private houses in Castle Avenue, to the south, but there is nothing to be seen.) Return along Dovecot Road and turn right into Saughton Road, continuing straight on for approximately 1 mile until a roundabout. Turn left along Calder Road and Gorgie Road, signposted city centre; after 0.5 miles turn right into Stenhouse Mill Lane, just after Shell filling station on the right side of Calder Road. A little way up the lane stands Stenhouse.

Structure

It was built, as a date above the entrance indicates, in 1623. On plan the structure shows a three-storeyed main block. From this main portion two wings projected; one, two-storeyed, was in continuation of the south gable, the other, which was carried a storey higher was centrally situated, and contained the entrance at its north re-entrant angle. The structure was harled, and was built of rubble, mainly freestone, with polished freestone quoins and dressings.

The gables throughout were crow-stepped and had moulded skew-puts; the chimney copes were also moulded.

Midway along the east lateral wall there were traces of a wing, which once projected eastwards to match the existing northern wing, and against the northern wing there had been a low building parallel to the northern portion of the main block.

Brief History

It was a property of the Stanhope family from 1511, but passed to Patrick Ellis, a prosperous merchant of Edinburgh, who extended an existing building in 1623

Stenhouse is used as a conservation centre, and can be viewed from the road.

Stenhouse

19 Baberton House (*)

Ordnance Survey (OSR) = NT 195696

Return to Gorgie Road (A71) and turn left, continuing along Calder Road until the third roundabout; turn left up Wester Hailes Road. At the next major junction (traffic lights) turn right into Westburn Road. Where Westburn Road bears left, turn off to right on to Baberton Road; just beyond Baberton Mains, a private lane turns left to Baberton House.

Structure

Sir James Murray built the original Kilbaberton in 1622. The main block was three storeys and a garret in height. It was laid out on a double L-plan, with two gabled, chimneyed wings projecting forwards to form a small south-facing courtyard with stair turrets in the angles.

Brief History

A charter of 1597 to John Elphinstone of the lands of "Kilbaberton" as resigned by Henry Wardlaw, specifies a tower. In 1612 there was a similar grant by the king to James and Martha Murray, which William Wardlaw of Kilbaberton had resigned; and in 1622 those lands were granted to James Murray, Master of the King's Works, and his spouse Katherine Weir.

It is said to have belonged to James VI and was a temporary residence of Charles X of France.

It is situated in private grounds and not accessible to the public. Permission to view the exterior should be made in writing.

Baberton House

20 Malleny House

Ordnance Survey (OSR) = NT 166667

Return to the junction of Westburn Road and Wester Hailes Road and turn right at the traffic lights; continue along Wester Hailes Road, through roundabout, until junction (traffic lights) with Lanark Road. Turn right on to Lanark Road (A70, signposted Balerno). Follow Lanark Road and Lanark Road West for 3 miles, and then turn left into Bridge Road, signposted Balerno. Just beyond Balerno High School on left, turn left into Bavelaw Road and take first turn on right into public car park. Return on foot to Bavelaw Road where the rear of Malleny House can be seen through the trees.

Structure
Malleny House, an extended 17th-century mansion with a round stair-tower, incorporates earlier work from at least 1589

Brief History
In the middle of the 17th century a branch of the Scotts of Murdieston held Malleny. It was sold in 1882 to the Earl of Rosebery.

Although occupied as a residence, the gardens are open all year under the care of The National Trust for Scotland. Admission.

Malleny House

21 Bavelaw Castle (*)

Ordnance Survey (OSR) = NT 168628

Turn right into Bavelaw Road and continue straight on past the SSPCA animal centre, bearing left at the next junction. Around 0.5 miles beyond the junction, turn left into the public car park. On leaving the car park on foot, turn left on road, cross Redford Bridge at Threipmuir Reservoir and walk up the steep hill between avenue of trees. Turn left at the junction at the top of hill and follow the road round bend to the right. Go through the gate leading to open land and the Pentland Hills and turn left; Bavelaw Castle (private estate) can be seen through the trees beyond the wall. After returning through the gate, the entrance to the castle can be seen within a few yards on the right.

Structure

Although restored it is mainly a 17th-century structure. On plan the house comprises a central main block and two wings. There are three storeys in height, the uppermost being an attic lit by dormers; the basement is vaulted. The walls were of rubble, rough-cast. The smaller windows had a bold roll-moulding at jamb and lintel; the larger had back-set margins. In the east re-entrant angle a modern circled turret was corbelled out above first-floor level on a heavy continuous corbelling of five members. The gables were crow-stepped; the roof was of timber and was slated.

The approach was from the east, and the entrance was placed almost midway along the east wall. Two tiers of gun-loops commanded it. It opened into the well of an internal wheel-stair, which was unusually situated in the building; through the stair-well the basement chambers were entered.

Bavelaw Castle

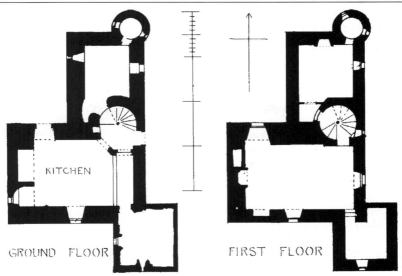

Bavelaw Castle – plans

Brief History

In 1628 the king granted to Laurence Scott of Harperrig, advocate, both Easter and Wester Bavelaw, with the tower and manor place, which Walter Dundas had resigned. Scott, in the same year, had to complain to the Privy Council regarding four men who, among other outrages, went to "the hous of Bavillaw whair I had raised twa turrets upoun the entrie thairof and covered the heads of the same with leid, and leddered the said turrets and rave doun and tooke away with thame and most pairt of the leid being upoun the said turrets for making of bullets and drapes to thair hacquebutts."

This is a private house, so please seek permission from the owners.

22 Lennox Castle (*)

Ordnance Survey (OSR) = NT 174671

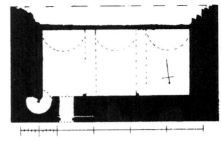

Lennox Castle – plan

Return to Balerno by the outward route and make way towards Edinburgh on Lanark Road West. After 1.25 miles, turn right (signposted Currie Kirk) opposite the turning for Riccarton Mains Road. Just after Currie Kirk an unmade road leads off to the right. After 0.75 miles Lymphoy House lies on the right; in the garden stands the ruin of Lennox Tower.

Structure

From the 15th century, the castle is rectangular on plan. The only window remaining has the typical 15th-century chamfer on jambs and lintel. The entrance is in the north wall at ground level. On the first floor was a single chamber, the hall, which had a large fireplace in the west gable and, in the north wall, a window with stone seats in the recess.

Brief History

It belonged to the earls of Lennox and was an occasional residence of Queen Mary and the Regent Morton, and a favourite hunting seat of James VI, from whom it passed into the possession of the celebrated George Heriot, who left money for the funding of Heriot's school in Edinburgh.

The tower stands in the ground of a private residence. A view of the ruin is by prior arrangement only.

Lennox Castle

23 Colinton Castle (*)

Ordnance Survey (OSR) = NT 216694

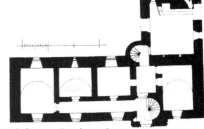

Colinton Castle – plan

Return by the same route to Lanark Road and turn right towards the city centre until the junction (traffic lights) with Wester Hailes Road and Gillespie Road. Turn right into Gillespie Road and continue for 1 mile through Colinton and along Bridge Road and Colinton Road to the entrance to Merchiston Castle School on the left. The ruin of Colinton Castle stands next to the headmaster's house in the grounds.

Structure

The building has been at least three storeys in height and is L-shaped on plan, the re-entrant angle opening to the north-west. The main block facing southwards is the original house. A later wing projected northwards having its eastern side in alignment with the east gable; contemporary with the wing was a circular stair-tower, which rose from the ground within the re-entrant angle, and gave access to all floors. The original staircase was on the south and pro-jected externally. The original ent-rance, a finely moulded door-piece with an empty panel-space above, was con-tained in this projection. Within the basement of the main block a vaulted passage running westward from the stair-well gave access to three vaulted cellars, and

there were two other vaulted cellars north and east of the stair, the northern latterly forming an access to the extension. The basement of the wing was vaulted, and was the kitchen.

Brief History

In 1531 James Foulis owned the lands of Colinton. Sir James Foulis of Colinton was returned heir to his father, James Foulis of Colinton, in 1609. He was King's Advocate in 1527. The house was occupied by Cromwell's soldiers during their operations round Edinburgh in 1650.

The ruin is currently in a dangerous state and is cordoned off. Visitors should report to Reception on arrival.

Colinton Castle

24 Craiglockhart Castle (*)

Ordnance Survey (OSR) = NT 226703

Return to school entrance and turn left along Colinton Road to the roundabout at the T-junction. Turn left down the continuation of Colinton Road then left at junction (traffic lights) into Craiglockhart Avenue. Take second turning on left into Craiglockhart Drive and after 0.25 miles bear right into Redhall House Drive; continue straight on and park near end of road. The remains of Redhall Castle lie on a fenced-off mound a short distance to the north of Redhall House. Return along Redhall House Drive and Craiglockhart Drive and turn right up Craiglockhart Drive. At junction (traffic lights) with Colinton Road, continue straight across into Glenlockhart Road where Craiglockhart Castle will be seen on the right soon after the junction.

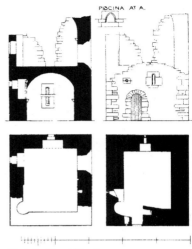

Craiglockhart Castle

Structure

The broken ruin has a wide outlook to north and west, but is not otherwise defensive.

In plan the structure is oblong and indications show that there were four storeys; two of theses were mezzanines formed within the barrel-vaults, which ceiled the basement and the floor above the Hall. The voids were chamfered at head and jambs. The entrance, which was in the north wall, had a semicircular head and was rebated for outer and inner doors; it was at ground level and opened directly into the basement. In the north-west angle a wheel-stair gave access to the mezzanine and upper floors. The wall-head would be surmounted by a parapet-walk, but it has not survived.

Brief History

In 1505 James IV granted to Thomas Kincaid, son of Thomas Kincaid, burgess of Edinburgh, on resignation by Patrick Kincaid of Craiglockhart, the lands of the same with tower and fortalice. In 1574 James Kincaid was in Craiglockhart.

It stands within Napier University grounds.

Craiglockhart Castle

25 Craighouse (*)

Ordnance Survey (OSR) = NT 234709

Continue along Glenlockhart Road for 0.75 miles, then turn left into Morningside Grove; at T-junction turn left into Craighouse Road and follow it round to the right. Park wherever possible immediately after the bend and proceed on foot up drive on left side of Craighouse Road to Old Craighouse (Napier University offices).

Structure

Craighouse is a plain three-storeyed oblong structure. Towards the western end of the north wall a rectangular stair-tower, carried one storey above the main block. The house was built of rubble and harled. The basement floor comprised two vaulted chambers. The wheel-stair was spacious and rose to the third floor, from which level access was given to the attic by a small turret-stair corbelled out within the west re-entrant angle.

Brief History

Laurence Symsone was returned heir to his father, Alexander Symsone of Craighouse in 1603. In 1685 it belonged to Sir Andrew Dick, son of Sir William Dick of Braid, who had been Provost of Edinburgh. Said to be haunted by the ghost of Jacky Gordon.

Used as offices, it is easily viewed from the drive.

Craighouse

26 Merchiston Castle (*)

Ordnance Survey (OSR) = NT 243717

Continue down Craighouse Road and along Myreside Road to junction (traffic lights) and turn right into Colinton Road. After almost 0.75 miles, Merchiston Castle (Napier University offices) can be seen on left, surrounded by campus buildings.

Merchiston Castle

Structure

The tower house of the Napiers of Merchiston is L-shaped on plan. Beneath the parapet walk were five main storeys and, above, it an attic within the roof space. The parapet, borne on separate corbels of two members, broke out into circled bartizans at the salient corners of the main block, but was merely rounded at the corners of the wing. Between the latter, however, could be seen the remains of a machiolation. The masonry was rubble, built in courses with chamfered dressings at such openings as have not been altered. The attic of the wing is lit by 17th-century dormer-windows.

No part of the tower itself had been vaulted, but in the re-entrant angle outside was a vaulted subterranean cellar reached by a stair descending from the basement of the wing and had two hatchways in its vault. Such provision is in every way unusual.

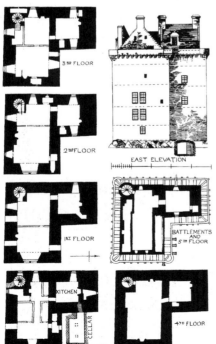

Brief History

The castle belonged from ancient times to the Napier family, three members of whom were successively Lord Provosts of the city in the times of James II and James III, and another the illustrious John Napier, the inventor of logarithms, who was born here in 1550. The castle figured prominently in the Douglas Wars and the civil strife during Queen Mary's reign.

There seems to be no objection to visitors viewing the exterior of the tower.

27 Bruntsfield House (*)

Ordnance Survey (OSR) = NT 252723

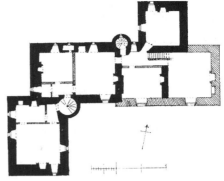

Continue along Colinton Road to junction (traffic lights) and cross straight over into Chamberlain Road, then follow road round bend to right to T-junction. Turn left along Strathearn Place to junction (traffic lights) and turn left into Whitehouse Loan. Take second turning on right into Warrender Park Road and take first right turning into Lauderdale Street. Bruntsfield House is on right at the south end of Lauderdale Street

Bruntsfield House – plan

Structure

As first built it was shaped on a Z-plan, comprising an oblong main block and two rectangular towers projecting from diametrically opposite corners. All three divisions held three storeys and an attic, the upper ones reached from two turret-stairs corbelled out within the north-west and south-east re-entrant angles. A courtyard is on the south, the arched entrance to which still existed although it had been considerably enlarged.

The masonry throughout was rubble, prepared for harling, with exposed dressings, which are rounded at the arris.

Brief History

This property takes its name from Richard Broune, King's Sergeant of the Muir, "Broune's field" becoming Bruntsfield by simple phonetic change. In 1381 Broune resigned the property to Sir Alan de Lauder,

Bruntsfield House

while in the 15th century it was with the Lauders of Hutton. For a short period it was forfeited to the Crown, but was restored to the same family. In 1603 it was sold to John Fairlie and his great-grandson sold the property in 1695 to George Warrender of Lochend, then a bailie and ultimately Lord Provost of Edinburgh, with whose descendants it remained until it was purchased by the municipality in 1935.

It is part of James Gillespie's High School; therefore viewing is by prior appointment.

28 Comiston House

Ordnance Survey (OSR) = NT 240687

Return along Lauderdale Street, and Warrender Park Road to junction (traffic lights) and turn right into Strathearn Place; at the end of Strathearn Place bear left and then right on to Church Hill. At T-junction (traffic lights) turn left and continue south on main road, along Morningside Road and then Comiston Road, for approximately 2 miles. Turn right into Camus Avenue and continue to end of street, at a small cul-de-sac on left side. In that cul-de-sac there is a footpath leading south to the remaining round tower of Comiston House.

Comiston House

Structure

All that survives of the old house of Comiston is a late 16ᵗʰ-century angle-tower of rubble, which had been incorporated in the south-east corner of the modern stables. The upper part was set out on corbelling, below which may be seen two oval gun-loops facing respectively north-east and south-east.

Brief History

The lands were held by Alexander de Meignes in 1355, but passed to Cunningham of Kilmaurs, then in 1531 to Foulis of Colinton, then to the Fairlies. In 1608 Comiston was held by the Creichs, then passed by marriage to the Cants, then again by marriage to the Porterfield family. The present house was built for Lord Provost James Forrester.

Can be viewed from the road.

29 Morton House (*)

Ordnance Survey (OSR) = NT 254679

Return along Camus Avenue and turn right up Comiston Road, continuing to a junction (traffic lights). Turn left along Frogston Road and after 0.25 miles turn right into Winton Drive then left into Winton Loan. Morton House can be seen through its gateway at the end of Winton Loan.

Structure

It is a little country house of Queen Anne's time, which seems to be based on the remains of an older building. In the early 18th century the house was L-shaped, the main block running north and south and a wing projecting east. The main block contained two storeys and an attic, while the wing, as the result of an alteration, had a storey less. The masonry was of rubble throughout, the window margins being back-set and chamfered.

Brief History

Robert the Bruce gave the property to the Sinclairs of Rosslyn in 1317. Thomas Rigg, High Sheriff of Edinburgh, owned the house about 1800. The current owners Lord and Lady Elliott bought it from the Trotters of Charterhall.

The house is a private residence, but can be seen from the road.

Morton House

30 Liberton Tower

Ordnance Survey (OSR) = NT 265697

Liberton Tower

Return along Winton Loan and Winton Road and turn left on to Frogston Road. At junction (traffic lights) turn right down Comiston Road. After 0.5 miles, fork right into Braid Road, continue for a further 0.5 miles, and then turn right along Braid Hills Drive. After rather more than 1.25 miles Liberton Tower can be seen on the left.

Structure

It is of typical 15th-century construction. Following a recent discovery of a draw hole above the main door, it proved that the access to the door was by a drawbridge on to a timber or stone stair. In the north-east corner of the hall is a drain for washing down the floor. Its location, together with the position of the main door and the garderobe, suggests that a timber screen to form a screens passage separated the north end of the hall. The form of the mural stairs at Liberton, which are made of stones built into the masonry like a straight stair bent into a curve, is not unusual, but is less common than the turnpike or spiral stair constructed from specially cut winders.

Brief History

Originally with the Dalmahoy family, they sold it to William Little, Lord Provost of Edinburgh, in 1587. He abandoned the tower on building the nearby Liberton House.

The tower is used as private holiday accommodation (Country Cottages in Scotland 0990 851133.) The owners are members of the Scottish Castles Association, and therefore the tower may be included in the Events Programme from time to time.

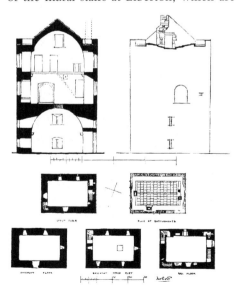

Liberton Tower —plans and section

31 Liberton House

Ordnance Survey (OSR) = NT 267694

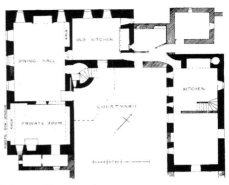

Liberton House – plan

Continue along Braid Hills Drive for a further 0.25 miles where Liberton House (occupied as a residence) lies a little back on the right side of the road.

Structure

A harled L-plan house built circa 1600 for the Littles of Liberton, who bought the estate in 1587. There are original window margins with rounded arrises. In the re-entrant angle is a round stair-turret corbelled out to the square at the second floor, its crow-stepped gable restored around 1890. Inside the porch is the original moulded entrance doorway of 1600, with an empty panel overhead. Unusually for a country house it opens not into the stair-turret but into the hall, but it is well guarded by gun loops

Brief History

It was a property of the Gilmours for 400 years, but was sold in 1976 and passed through many developers with plans for hotels and country clubs. Nicholas Groves-Raines

bought it from a nursing home and, following years of hard work, the family moved in, in February 1994.

It is a private residence, but access to the gardens and exterior of the house can be arranged privately by telephoning 0131 467 7777. The owners are members of the Scottish Castles Association, and therefore the tower may be included in the Events Programme from time to time.

Liberton House

32 Inch House (*)

Ordnance Survey (OSR) = NT 278709

Continue along Braid Hills Drive to junction (traffic lights); turn left down Liberton Brae and continue straight on through first junction (traffic lights) into Liberton Road. At next junction (traffic lights) turn right on to Gilmerton Road then, after less than 0.25 miles, take first turning on left signposted Liberton School and Inch Park. Fork left and follow road through park to Inch House.

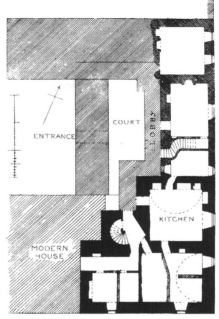

Inch House – plan

Structure
The original house forms the eastern angle of the present mansion. It was an L-plan of three storeys and an attic. The old building is of rubble and is rough-cast. The gables were crow-stepped and the chimney copes moulded. The stair-tower terminated in a crenellated parapet above a continuous moulded corbel-table.

Inch House can be viewed externally from within the park.

Brief History
James Winrame of Nether Liberton (founder of Inch House), was keeper of the Great Seal in 1623.

Inch House

33 Craigmillar Castle

Ordnance Survey (OSR) = NT 288709

Return to Gilmerton Road, turn left, continue for just over 0.5 miles and turn left at traffic lights into Kingston Avenue. At T-junction turn right along Old Dalkeith Road, then take first left turning on to Craigmillar Castle Road. After 0.5 miles turn left into car park for Craigmillar Castle.

Structure

Crowning the brow of a gentle eminence, it commands a magnificent view. It consisted of a lofty square keep, an inner court and a quadrangular embattled wall with circular corner towers; the whole surrounded by an outer rampart or, in places, a moat. The newer part to the west was added in 1661; the keep must be older than 1427, but much of the building was reared most likely after its burning by Hertford in 1544. Within are the noisome dungeons, in whose partition wall a skeleton was found bricked up (1813); the kitchen, with mighty oven; Queen Mary's bower and a barrel-vaulted roof.

Brief History

The name of this place occurs in a charter of mortification granted in 1212 by William, son of Henry de Craigmillar. Later it belonged to John de Capella, and from him Sir Simon Preston, whose descendants retained it for nearly three centuries, purchased it in 1374. James III imprisoned his brother John, Earl of Mar, here in 1478; and James V was sent here during his minority. Queen Mary, after returning in 1561, made Craigmillar a frequent residence, and here her divorce from Darnley was mooted. James VI planned his matrimonial excursion to Denmark.

It is in the care of Historic Scotland and open April to Sept. daily and Oct. to March from Saturday to Wednesday. Admission charge. Tel 0131 661 4445.

Craigmillar Castle

34 Peffermill House

Ordnance Survey (OSR) = NT 284717

Continue down Craigmillar Castle Road to junction (traffic lights) and turn left into Peffermill Road; after just over 0.25 miles, Peffermill House can be seen standing back from the road, on the right.

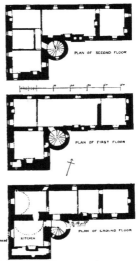

Structure

Edward Edgar built it around 1636. On plan the structure is L-shaped, comprising a main block and a jamb. In the re-entrant angle is a circled staircase tower. It is three storeys including the attic, and a garret above. The masonry is built of rubble, harled with the dressings exposed. The gables were crow-stepped.

Peffermill House – plan

Brief History

In 1661 Peffermill was bought by Sir John Gilmour, and remained with that family's trust until 1982, when Nicholas and Limma Groves-Raines acquired it. They restored and transformed both the house and garden and lived there until 1995. Peffermill is said to be the house Sir Walter Scott described as Dumbiedykes in "The Heart of Midlothian"

It is a private residence, but the owners are very accommodating with visitors who introduce themselves. The owners are members of the Scottish Castles Association, and the Events Programme may include Peffermill House from time to time .

Peffermill House

35 Brunstane House (*)

Ordnance Survey (OSR) = NT 316725

Brunstane House – plan

Return along Peffermill Road and cross the junction (traffic lights) into Niddrie Mains Road. After just over 1 mile turn left at junction (traffic lights) into Duddingston Park South, continuing for almost 0.75 miles to a roundabout. Turn right on to Milton Road and continue for 0.5 miles; at large roundabout, continue straight on then immediately take first right turn into Brunstane Road South. Continue for 0.5 miles to Brunstane House which can been seen through its gateway on left.

Structure

On plan it forms three sides of a square. The north-eastern angle contained masonry which may date from the 16th century; incorporating this nucleus a new house was erected in 1639 by John Maitland, second Earl of Lauderdale, on an L-plan. Comprising a main block and a wing; within the re-entrant angle the present semi-octagonal tower projected and housed a spacious wheel-stair on which the entrance opened.

Brief History

The house, once known as Gilberton, belonged to the Crichtons, who also possessed Brunston in Penicuik. As Gilberton, belonging to the laird of Brunston, the house was ordered by the Privy Council in 1547 to be cast down because the laird, Alexander Crichton, had given assistance to English invaders. By 1609 the property had passed from the Crichtons to the Maitlands, and the date 1639 denoted the first reconstruction.

Private residence, but can be seen from the road. If you wish to enter the grounds please telephone 0131 669 6430, or ring the doorbell.

Brunstane House

36 Craigentinny House (*)

Ordnance Survey (OSR) = NT 290747

Return along Brunstane Road South and turn left on to Milton Road. At first roundabout, turn right on to Sir Harry Lauder Road and continue for approximately 1.5 miles until a roundabout. Turn left into Portobello Road, and then take first right turning into Wakefield Avenue, continuing on to Craigentinny Road. After rather more than 1 mile, turn left into Loaning Road where Craigentinny House can be seen on the right, close to the road.

Structure

The original comprised an oblong main block of four storeys running east and west and a wing on the south, which contained a scale-and-platt stair. This stair rose to the second storey and had a chamber above it, but the latter was removed to allow the scale-stair to continue upwards, and so replace a turret-stair part of which still exists within the east re-entrant angle although the steps themselves have been removed. The stair-turret is set out on a conoidal corbelling above the first floor and is divided horizontally by a string course, the upper part, capped with a conical roof, containing a gun-loop facing east. Beside the turret was a projection for the hall chimney, which was also set out on corbelling. In all parts of the building the masonry is random rubble with freestone dressings, rounded at the arris. The majority of the openings are built with relieving arches.

Brief History

James Nisbet, a descendant of Henry Nisbet owned the property in the late 16th/early 17th centuries.

The house is used as council offices, but can be seen from the road.

Craigentinny House

37 Lochend House (*)

Ordnance Survey (OSR) = NT 273743

Continue along Loaning Road to T-junction and turn right into Restalrig Road South (one way), then first left into Marionville Road. At roundabout turn right into Lochend Road South then take first left turning into Lochend Park; park car just after turning and enter public park on left. Lochend House stands on a low crag on the east side of Lochend Loch and the earliest parts of the building can be seen through the trees on the crag's edge. On returning to the car note the doocot close to the park entrance.

Structure

All that is left is a much-altered rubble-built fragment attached to the west side of a modern house. This older part has had two storeys, the lower of which was once vaulted. The only surviving features of interest are a large kitchen-fireplace, within an external projection, and a small chamber-fireplace, both maybe of the 16th century.

Brief History

The lands of Restalrig were possessed by the Logans early in the 14th century, and remained in their hands till the early part of the 17th century when Robert Logan forfeited them on account of his connection with the Gowrie Conspiracy.

Can be seen from within the park.

Lochend House

38 Pilrig House (*)

Ordnance Survey (OSR) = NT 265757

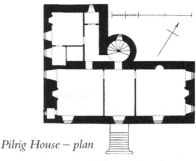

Pilrig House – plan

Return to Lochend Road South and turn left; continue for 0.5 miles to roundabout, cross straight over to Duke Street and at next junction (traffic lights) continue straight to Great Junction Street. At next junction with traffic lights, turn left on to Bonnington Road. After less than 0.25 miles, turn left into Pilrig House Close at the end is Pilrig House.

Structure

It is L-shaped on plan and three storeys in height, the uppermost floor being an attic formed partly in the roof space. The main block runs east and west, while the wing extended north in continuation of the west gable. The re-entrant angle opened to the north-east and contained a stair tower, circular below but corbelled out to a rectangle above the stair-head, where it contained a little upper chamber.

The masonry was harled rubble, with dressed and back-set margins. The gables were crow-stepped, and the roof has been renewed.

The central part of the south side was carried above the main wall-head in a curvilinear gablet with scrolled skew-puts, which was evidently added about the end of the 17th century.

Brief History

In 1623 Gilbert Kirkwood acquired the lands of Pilrig from the Monypenny family; and, 15 years later, when he came to build his house, he probably incorporated some part of an earlier building. James Balfour, merchant in Leith, then acquired the estate of Pilrig in 1718.

The house is occupied as flats, but the building can be seen from the road.

Pilrig House

39 Inchgarvie

Ordnance Survey (OSR) = NT 137795

Because of its remoteness it is not included in the Edinburgh route.

Structure

Not much remains of the 15th-century castle, to which James IV added a stronger tower in 1513. It was altered in later centuries, and used as a prison for a time.

Brief History

It was a property of the Dundas family from 1491, and used by Royalists in the 1650s. It was re-fortified against John Paul Jones, a Scotsman who entered the American navy in 1775 and harried shipping in British waters during the American War of Independence; then again in the 20th century against German bombers trying to destroy the Forth Bridge.

The ruins can be seen from the bridge or from North Queensferry.

Inchgarvie

Castle Touring Guides

East Lothian (East)

Map 2 – East Lothian (East)

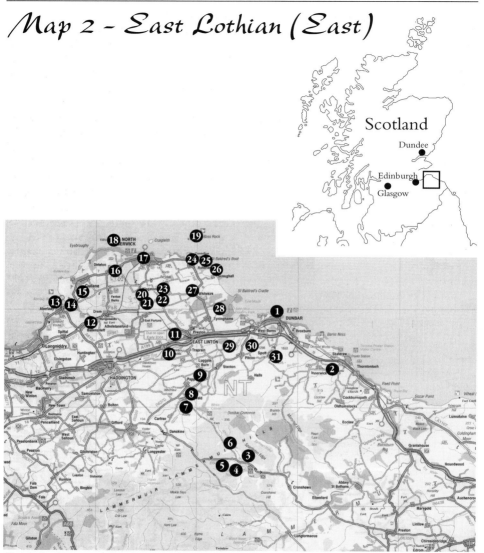

© Philip's 2003, © Crown copyright 2003

1 Dunbar Castle

Ordnance Survey (OSR) = NT 678794

A1087 from the west – to the centre of Dunbar, and turn left at the mini roundabout, OR A1087 from the south – to the centre of Dunbar, straight on at the mini roundabout. Turn right at the next mini roundabout, with Castle Hotel (Black Agnes) on the right. Turn left into the Leisure Pool car park and walk down the path; or take the next left turn and drive through the narrow streets and park overlooking the harbour.

Structure

The remains appear to be those of a castle with gatehouse and a walled enceinte. The masonry is of the local freestone like that of the neighbouring quarries, ashlar faced and rubble cored. The gatehouse is of a 15th century type and is what is left of the "barbican" then erected. The numerous gunloops are evidence of a late date. The isolated battery is inaccessible for the connecting passage is broken. It was further reduced to make way for the Victoria Harbour in 1844.

Brief History

The castle covered the most convenient landing on the coast beyond Berwick, and after Berwick became finally English in 1483, that importance was intensified for Scotland. It dates back to the 12th century when it was a Cockspatrick family stronghold. The present ruins do not quite represent either the castle over which a battle was fought with the army of Edward I in 1297. Edward II sheltered here after the Battle of Bannockburn in 1314. Its most famous event when it was defended against the Earl of Salisbury for five months in 1338 by "Black" Agnes, Countess of Dunbar. On the latter occasion the place was blockaded on the seaside by two great galleys and other smaller ships, but Sir Alexander Ramsay, on a stormy night, slipped through in a vessel from the Bass with food and reinforcements. On the orders of Parliament it was destroyed in 1488.

When war occurred in 1496, James IV found it advisable again to construct a castle at Dunbar. In the next reign, Dunbar Castle was possessed by John, Duke of Albany, "Governor of Scotland", during the minority of James V. In 1547, the English considered the occupation of Dunbar as an alternative to Haddington, and it was later urged by Lord

Dunbar Castle

Grey that "a great part of Dunbar town is beyond danger of shot, and if fortified, may irynge the castle and some part mak it".

Begun in 1559 the castle was re-fortified by the French, but later destroyed.

It was to the castle that Queen Mary fled in 1566 from the murderers of Rizzio, her secretary, and again in 1567 following the murder of Darnley. Mary's third husband Bothwell came to Dunbar having escaped from Carberry Hill.

Freely accessible, but many parts are barred as they are in a dangerous condition.

Details on the town of Dunbar are on page 208.

Dunbar Castle

2 Innerwick Castle (*)

Ordnance Survey (OSR) = NT 735737

Take the A1087 south from Dunbar, and join the A1 after 1.9 miles. Take the second right turn to Innerwick; go over the railway bridge and through the village of Crowhill. Turn left to Innerwick, but ignore the next right turn to Innerwick. Shortly there is a Z bend, with a little space to park. Walk through the gate opposite a house called Castledene.

Structure

This ruin stands on top of a sandstone outcrop, on the left bank of the Thornton Burn, and overhanging the Thornton ravine. The deep but narrow channel of the burn skirts a harder mass of rock to form a promontory encompassed on the north, east and south by the loop of the stream. The promontory is entirely covered with building of different periods.

Only the lowest storey of the castle remains, but important features such as accesses have disappeared. However the arrangement of the plan does not seem to warrant a date earlier than the 15th century for the oldest structures.

The main block comprised two chambers of approximately equal length, but unequal in width, with a vaulted passage on the north. These chambers were ceiled with round barrel-vaults and entered from the east, the northern through a vestibule within the thickness of the wall, the southern from a passage, at the southern end of which are traces of a staircase leading to the upper floor. In the east wall of these chambers above the vault was a stone conduit sloping diagonally downwards in the thickness of the wall, which may have served to collect roof water for domestic purposes.

A rib-vaulted passage on the north turns southwards along the main block and gave access to a long apartment running east and west. The western portion, nearest the passage, had a large fireplace beside the doorway and was elevated above the eastern and larger division. This chamber was covered with a round barrel-vault but appears to be later than the main block. Off it, at its eastern end, was a little room on the north, which had been ceiled in wood, while a doorway farther west led to an irregularly shaped chamber with a drain in the north wall east

Innerwick Castle

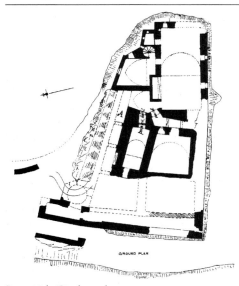

Innerwick Castle – plan

and a smoke screen for, when the Duke of Albany arrived with a large Scots' army to save Innerwick and Cocklaw, Percy and Douglas had headed south-west to contact Douglas vassals and march on Wales.

In 1547 the English attacked Innerwick during the wars of the 'Rough Wooing'. This was when the English insisted, by force, that the child Mary, Queen of Scots, (1542-1587) be married to the English Prince Edward.

The castle of Innerwick was used by Scots horsemen in 1650 as a base to attack Cromwell's supply lines, in conjunction with the raids made by the 'desperado gallants' of Tantallon Castle, and the 'moss troopers' of Dirleton Castle.

Freely accessible.

of the window. This chamber had a pointed barrel-vault and gave access to a small circular staircase. The structures west of the main block are extremely ruinous. The entrance must have been by a stairway abutting against the oblong tower and descending to the north passage

Brief History

Little is known except that it belonged successively to families of the name of Stewart and Hamilton, ancestors of the Earls of Haddington. In 1403 Innerwick was besieged by the English knight 'Hotspur' Percy and Archibald, 4th Earl of Douglas, a Scot held by the Percys after the defeat of the Scots army at the battle of Homildon Hill, near Wooler, in 1402. However the siege of Innerwick and its near neighbour Cocklaw tower, a Gladstone house, proved to be a mock affair

Innerwick Castle

3 Gamelshiel Castle (*)

Ordnance Survey (OSR) = NT 649648

Retrace your steps to the A1, turn right, and travel south for 5.5 miles. In Grantshouse, turn right on the A6112 to Duns/Coldstream. Enjoy the view for a further 7.5 miles, passing a turn to Eden Hills Broch en route (long walk), and on entering Preston turn right on the B6355 and follow all successive signs to Cranshaws. (Pass Cranshaw Smiddy Tea Rooms). Towards the end of the reservoir on your left, you can park in or at the Fishery Car Park. It is a 20-minute walk to Gamelshiel.

Structure

The ruins of Gamelshiel can be found on the left bank of Hall Burn. The portions of building upon it consist of part of the north and south walls of a small tower. The walls are mainly built of whinstone in narrow courses. The basement floor had been vaulted.

Brief History

In 1505 John Forrest succeeded his father John Forrest in the lands of "Gamelshields". In 1679 James Home entered upon the lands of Wester "Gamelshields" as heir to his father George Home of Gamelshields. The superior of the lands was Hepburn of Hailes.

"There was a traditional story of the lady who was killed by a prowling wolf when taking her evening stroll near her stately home. Her husband buried her mangled corpse in the corner of the courtyard, and ever after, till death sent him to rejoin her in another world, he sat at his chamber window looking through his tears over her grave; her soul as dark as the forest shades around him, and his voice as mournful as their autumn music." – Weekly Scotsman 5th August 1899.

Freely accessible

Gamelshiel Castle

4 Penshiel Grange (*)

Ordnance Survey (OSR) = NT 642632

> Further on the main road (0.25 miles), turn left towards Priestlaw Farm, and then turn right to Penshiel. It is then a 15-minute walk.

Structure

On a plateau under the east shoulder of Penshiel Hill, and on the left bank of the Faseny Water, near its junction with the Whiteadder, are the vaulted ruins of a grange, part of which still remains, which was attached to Melrose Abbey. There are relics of a tower, and probably a staircase at the south-east corner. The main building was built of large reddish boulders. The ground floor was vaulted transversely and was lit by two small windows in each gable. The entrance was in the north wall, and three crossbars secured the doorway. To the south of this building was a courtyard enclosed by a stone wall, and to the north were foundations of two buildings, probably of a later date.

The grange farm must have been itself an imposing structure. The whole ground floor had been vaulted transversely. To the south of this building was a large courtyard enclosed by a wall.

Brief History

Penshiel is referred to in a charter granted by the Earl of Dunbar to the monks of the Isle of May in 1200. Later John Fitz Michael granted lands to Melrose Abbey, east of that given to the Priory of the Isle of May. The main building described above was possibly erected in the first half of the 15th century. The lands of Penshiel were included in the gift of the Melrose lands in 1621 to Thomas Hamilton, Earl of Melrose, afterwards Earl of Haddington.

> Freely accessible, but contact Clegg, Kennedy, Drew on 01361 890665 before any visit

Penshiel Grange

5 Mayshiel

Ordnance Survey (OSR) = NT 622641

Return to the B6355 and turn left. Mayshiel is a further 1.4 miles on your left and can be seen from the road.

Structure

It is believed to date from the 15th century, but is now modernised. The name literally means the shieling or shelter of the May.

Brief History

The property was made over by John Fitz Michael to the priory of the Isle of May. From the Register of Pittenweem, up to 1631, it was feued out to William Cockburn of that ilk. In 1634 the lands of Mayshiel came into the possession of Thomas Lord Fenton, and 14 years later his son, Alexander, Knight of Kellye was served heir to the property. Alexander was with the army which marched with Charles II on his invasion of England in 1651, and having been taken prisoner after the Battle of Worcester, was sent to the Tower of London. In the Sasine Records of 1794, Mayshiel was resigned by Isobel Knox and Thomas Pringle her spouse. Thereafter there is a record of a succession of Knoxs as proprietors. In 1815 Archibald Knox disponed Mayshiel to William Cunningham, and he sold the estate to Governor Alexander Houstoun of Clerkington. The Houstouns occupied the property during the 19th century, and the family found pleasure in occasional residence in "the auld hoose".

View from the road. Contact Clegg, Kennedy, Drew on 01361 890665, for access to photograph.

Mayshiel

6 Johnscleugh (*)

Ordnance Survey (OSR) = NT 631665

> Return on the B6355 back towards the reservoir. Turn left to Garvald. Johnscleugh is about 1.3 miles on your right.

Structure

This 17th-century dwelling house on the left bank of the Whiteadder Water is oblong on plan. A semicircular tower projecting from the middle of the south wall contained a wheel stair, which gave access to the upper floor. There were originally two apartments on the ground floor with barrel-vaulted ceilings, but the eastern chamber had been subdivided by a partition, and the vault removed. The building contained two storeys beneath the wall head and a garret within the roof, but could have been lowered which would explain the lack of gable crow-steps.

Brief History

The lands of "Johniscleuch" in 1598 were granted to George Lauder of the Bass, but later were seized for debt; and in 1634 the creditors' process was assigned to Richard Lauder of Halton. He had a royal charter of confirmation of these and other lands formerly belonging to the Lauders of the Bass.

> View from the road.

Johnscleugh

7 Nunraw (*)

Ordnance Survey (OSR) = NT 597706

Continue on the minor road for 4.25 miles, passing the White Castle Iron Age Fort. Turn through a low arch on the right, which is the entrance to Nunraw

Structure

It is mainly modern, but there is a medieval nucleus, built about the middle of the 15th century as a peelhouse or fortalice, overlaid and obscured by a mid 19th-century restoration and addition save at the northeastern angle, where a late 16th-century tower rises above the stable court. The portion of the main building which lies south of this tower is outwardly modern, but its arrangement on plan suggests that it is contemporary with the tower and also that the original structure was built on a Z-plan.

The building is four storeys in height below a continuous parapet walk. That the square projecting towers should have parapet walks is usual in the period. On the ground floor the main block had a vaulted passage running longitudinally from the west staircase against the south wall to a doorway in the east wall. The two lowest floors of the tower are vaulted.

Brief History

In 1547, when an English invasion was imminent, Elizabeth, Prioress of Haddington, undertook to the Privy Council "the cuire and keeping of the place and fortalice of Nunraw", with an obligation to keep the same "fra our auld ynemeis of Ingland and all utharis", and deliver it to nobody without the Governor's command, or raze it if there was no alternative. Nevertheless Nunraw fell into the hands of Lord Grey of Wilton and was kept for the English by the laird of Brunstone.

The estate of Nunraw was alternatively known as Whitecastle and was transferred by Elizabeth Hepburn, the last prioress of the nunnery of Haddington, to the Hepburns of Beanston, a branch of the Hailes family. In 1595 Patrick Hepburn of Whitecastle and Helen Cockburn his wife are on record; and in 1615 Patrick Hepburn, alias Nunraw. This Patrick of Beanston and Whitecastle, in 1617,

Nunraw

granted to his son John, on the occasion of his marriage, various lands including Easter and Wester Nunraw. Pat Hepburn of Nunraw is on the list of heritors in East Lothian in 1685 preserved among the estate papers at Eaglescairnie.

Nunraw House is the Abbey Guesthouse. Accessibility and hospitality are part of the situation. Visitors are welcome. Tel: 01620 830228 (guest house) or website liamdevlin.tripod.com/nunraw/

Nunraw

8 Stoneypath Tower (*)

Ordnance Survey (OSR) = NT 596714

Return to the main road, and turn right. In Garvald turn right to the church, and follow the Stenton sighs. Turn right on the B6370, and then turn right again to Stenton. Turn right and then right again at the Stoneypath Tower sign. The Tower is at the end of the minor road.

Structure

The ruin of this 15th-century tower is situated to the east north east of Garvald village on the right bank of a ravine traversed by the Papana Water below its confluence with the Thorter Burn. The building is L-shaped on plan, and between the first floor and wall head levels were apparently three storeys, the uppermost ceiled with a stone vault. The walls are built of roughly coursed rubble with dressed corners. On a quoin at the southwest angle was a shield rudely incised with the arms of the Lyle family. On the west wall of the main block there was a projection with a window to the south and a machiolated opening beneath, which could hardly have been defensive and probably was a garderobe.

The entrance was in the south wall at the first floor level, where a breach in the wall had been built up and a modern doorway inserted. The basement of the main block contained one apartment, with a chamber of similar dimensions in the mezzanine floor above. Mural chambers were placed in the lateral walls and a narrow window in the east wall. The greater portion of the vaulted ceiling has fallen, filling the chamber with its debris. The wing contained two chambers at this level.

The hall occupied the full extent of the first floor of the main block. It had a large fireplace in the east wall with a sink and drain on the south lighted by a small window. A window on the north had stone seats and a cupboard in the western jamb. On crossing the hall the wheel-stair, somewhat unusually situated in the north wall of the main wing, was reached. It communicated with the basement and the upper floors.

Stoneypath Tower

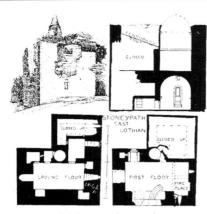

Stoneypath Tower – plans and section

Brief History

John Lyle of Stoneypath is on record as early as 1446 in a charter by James II to Robert de Lyle of Duchal. In 1494 "David Lile of Stanepeth" was pursuing the free tenants of Duns in a case of multure to the mill of Duns, which he had feued. The Lisles continued there for more than a century thereafter. In 1609 George "Lyell" was of "Stanypeth", and had a charter of novodamus to himself, his wife Agnes Hamilton and their son and heir George, which included also their estates in Berwickshire, but this followed, in the same year, by a resignation of the property and its transference to Alexander Hamilton of Innerwick.

Later (1616) the property was conferred upon Archibald Douglas of Whittingeham, when it was specified as having been part of the earldom of March, and in 1628 was in possession of William Douglas of "Stanypeth". His daughter married Arthur Douglas, nephew of the 8th Earl of Morton, and to this Arthur and his wife Stoneypath was conveyed with the barony of Whittinghame. In this way Stoneypath came ultimately to the Setons from whom in time it passed by purchase.

> The castle is clearly visible, but undergoing restoration. Entry to the site is not possible. The owner is a member of the Scottish Castles Association, and the Events Programme may include Stoneypath Tower from time to time.

Stoneypath Tower

9 Whittinghame Tower (*)

Ordnance Survey (OSR) = NT 602733

> Return to the Stoneypath Tower sign and turn left. Turn left on the B6370, and over the bridge to Papple. Turn right and right again to Whittinghame

Structure

A late 15th or early 16th-century tower close to the ravine through which flows the Whittinghame Water. On plan the structure is L-shaped, while the square wing projects, not from a lateral wall as is usual, but from the north gable and contains the entrance and the staircase, which is rectangular on the lower flights and circular above. It is a picturesque entrance doorway, with large bead and hollow mouldings. There are three storeys beneath the wall head, which terminates in a corbel course surmounted by a walk with a crenellated parapet, which returns round the whole building. A garret over the main block is entered from the parapet walk.

The basement chamber was modernized but retained its stone vaulted ceiling, below which a mezzanine floor was entered off the staircase but was removed. The windows have been enlarged, and direct access with the exterior provided in the east wall.

Brief History

Whittinghame was part of the great historical possessions of the earls of March, until in 1372 George of Dunbar, 10th Earl of March, conferred the lands on Sir James Douglas of Dalkeith, who had married his sister Agnes and was the founder of the Collegiate Church of Dalkeith. His son became first Lord Dalkeith and his grandson, on marrying a daughter of James I, first Earl of Morton. The fourth Earl was the Regent Morton and it was at Whittinghame that the proposal for the assassination of Darnley was made to him by Bothwell and Lethington in January 1567, beneath a yew tree. On his execution and forfeiture in 1581, title and lands lapsed to

Whittinghame Tower

Whittinghame Tower – coat of arms

daughter of Sir Archibald Douglas of Whittinghame and heiress of her brother Archibald, and again by marriage with Kingston's only surviving daughter to the Hon. William Hay of Drummelzier, son of the first Earl of Tweeddale, remaining with the Hays till it was sold in 1817, along with Stoneypath to James Balfour.

The 4th Earl of Balfour died on June 27th 2003 aged 77, and he was once the only viscount to be an able seaman in the Merchant Navy. The earldom was created in 1922 for the former Tory Prime Minister Arthur Balfour. Prior to that, the Balfours had been lairds of Balbirnie in Fife for generations.

the Crown, but were later returned to the representative of the family. Whittinghame passed in 1660 to Alexander Seton first Lord Kingston, who had married Elizabeth,

Private property. Permission should be sought from the owner.

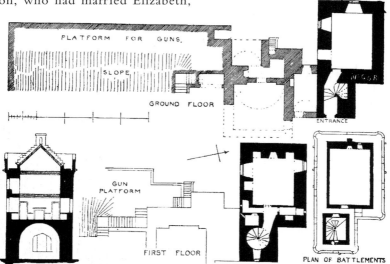

Whittinghame Tower – plans and section

10 Hailes Castle (*)

Ordnance Survey (OSR) = NT 575758

Return to the main road. Turn right and left at the roundabout to East Linton. Through Luggate follow the East Linton signs. Turn left in Traprain to Kippilaw. Then turn left at the small T-junction and the entrance is 0.5 miles along the road.

Structure

The castle consisted of an outer and inner ward encompassed by walls of enceinte, which have been strengthened with towers at intervals; between these towers the curtain was embodied in a later building. At the junction of the outer and inner wards there were, on the south, indications of a circular tower with a projection external to the wall of enceinte, which to the west of this was salient. In this portion of the wall, where it faced due south, the remains of the arched principal entrance were found.

The masonry of the mid tower, where it had not been rebuilt, was of large cubical blocks of reddish freestone ashlar diagonally axed, but the dressings and mouldings had been polished. A heavy basement course returned along the north wall of the mid tower and probably continued along the curtain. The masonry of the curtains on the south and west is dissimilar and inferior.

The north-west tower is quadrangular and contained five storeys beneath the wall head; the outer walls still stand but in a ruinous state. A wheel-stair, of which traces can still be seen, occupied the north-east angle.

The large tower midway along the north curtain was incomplete in that the south and the greater portion of the east wall are missing. The exterior of the north gable was divided into two tiers by a string-course, which returned above the head of the window.

The north curtain and the towers are coeval and date from the 13th century.

Brief History

It belonged from a very early period to the Hepburns, and the more modern parts to the time of the famous James Hepburn, Earl of Bothwell, Queen Mary's husband.

In February 1548 Lord Grey of Wilton had the place delivered to him and wrote "The

Hailes Castle

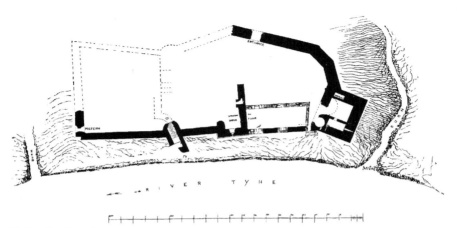

Hailes Castle – plan

house is for the bignes, of suche excellent bewtie within, as I have seldom sene any in Englande except the Kinges Majesties, and of verie good strengthe". Thereafter Hugh Douglas with fifty men held it for the English invaders. This was apparently Hugh Douglas of Longniddry.

In the care of Historic Scotland and therefore open at all reasonable times. Telephone 0131 6688800.

Hailes Castle

11 Markle (*)

Ordnance Survey (OSR) = NT 579775

Return to the minor road to East Linton. Turn left to East Linton and cross the A1. Go under the bridge and turn left, and then first right before the railway bridge. Take the B1377 and after 0.5 miles turn left to Markle. Go over the railway line and turn left into Markle Fisheries. There are parking facilities.

Structure

The outcrop has been surrounded by a ditch, flanked by outer and inner ramparts, to form an enclosure. The east gable still stands to its complete height, but the other walls are fragmentary. The gable had been heightened to receive a very acutely pitched roof. The masonry suggests that the structure has either been built out of old material or that it had become so ruinous that a complete reconstruction was necessary.

The bank against which the structure was built, runs north–north–east and south–south–west and appears to have been walled, with circled towers projecting northwards at the north-eastern portion, and to have had cross walls running from it south-eastwards. Between the cross walls are the ruins of a second structure, which was at least three storeys in height, of 16th century date and oblong in plan.

At the northern end of this wall there is a stone channel widening internally, which was an inlet for water; adjoining it to the south were the remains of a cupboard recess; the north wall had contained a kitchen fireplace. The upper storey had a wooden floor. A window and a small recess were the only features at this level.

Brief History

There was a chapel at Markle or "Merkill" dedicated to S. Mary, the patronage of which was associated ingrants with that of the church of Linton or Prestonkirk. Alan of "Merkshulle" was an archer serving "Peter de Lubant" as English commander with other men from East Lothian in Livingstone Peel in 1312. Markle is in the list of places burnt in 1401 and again in Hertford's invasion of 1544.

As described above, but a courtesy call at the Angling centre next to the car park would be appreciated.

Markle

12 Ballencrieff House

Ordnance Survey (OSR) = NT 487783

> From Markle return to the B1377 and turn left. Keep on the B1377 through East Fortune and Drem. Ballencrieff is 1.5 miles past Drem on the left hand side.

Structure

The structure was erected in 1586. On plan the mansion is oblong, the south-western portion is the original and contained three storeys beneath its wall head with an attic storey lit by dormer windows in the roof.

Brief History

King Robert the Bruce in 1307 confiscated the lands of Ballencrieff from Henry de Pinkney, Lord of Ballencrieff and Keeper of Berwick Castle, and gifted them to his esquire, Maurice Murray.

For the next 600 years the Murrays, a famous border family, continuously held the property. In 1507, James IV commanded James Murray (his private secretary) to build himself a fortified house at Ballencrieff. This was carried out and that gentleman, along with his king, died at the Battle of Flodden in 1513.

The house was destroyed in or around 1545 during the time of 'The Rough Wooing'. In 1586 another John Murray rebuilt the castle and brought his bride Margarete Hamilton to the house in that year. His family crest features above the main doorway.

Sir Gideon Murray bought the castle from his nephew John in 1615. Sir Gideon was Depute Treasurer for Scotland for King James VI. He added the famous heraldic ceiling to the Great Hall in 1617. Charles I in 1643 created his son Patrick Murray, a keen royalist, 1st Lord Elibank.

Between 1703 and 1721, five famous brothers were born in the castle, each eminent in forming the history of the times. One, Patrick, the 5th Lord was a friend to Dr Samuel Johnson and James Boswell, both of whom he entertained here in 1773. Another, General James Murray was born in 1721 and became the first British Governor of Canada in 1763.

Inhabitants of the castle have also witnessed significant events in Scotland's history, including the Battle of Prestonpans in 1745.

In 1868 the property accidentally burnt down. Restoration began in 1992 by Peter Gillies and his partner Lin Dalgleish, and was completed in summer 1997 – some 690 years after King Robert presented the lands to his trusted servant.

> This restored house can be viewed from the highway. It is an ideal venue for a small wedding (Tel 01875 870784, email info@ballencrieff-castle.com or web www.ballencrieff-castle.com).

Ballencrieff House

13 Kilspindie Castle (*)

Ordnance Survey (OSR) = NT 462801

From Ballencrieff continue on the B1377 for 0.5 miles, and then turn right on the A6137 to Aberlady. At the junction turn right on the A198 to North Berwick and then turn immediately left to Kilspindie Golf Club. Park and walk on the path. The scant ruins are to your left.

Structure

The remains are fragmentary and consist of the north wall, which is never higher than a few feet, containing the entrance and a gunloop, and the return of the west wall.

Brief History

In 1561 it is recorded that "Aberlady teind and ferme wes set of auld to Archibald Douglas of Kilspindie". Aberlady was the property of the bishopric of Dunkeld and in 1612 there was a royal confirmation of a grant of these lands by the bishop, with consent of his chapter, to Alexander Hay, Clerk-register, including "the castell toure and fortalice biggit be Patrick Douglas of Kilspindie upon the north part of the saidis landis of Abirladie towards the sey"; and of infeftmants by Hay in favour of Patrick Douglas, junior, son of the builder of the tower and son-in-law to Hay. The tower is therefore of a date in the later part of the 16th century.

Freely accessible.

Kilspindie Castle

14 Luffness House (*)

Ordnance Survey (OSR) = NT 476804

> Continue from Kilspindie on the A198 for nearly 1 mile and Luffness House is on your right set well above the road.

Structure

It was T-shaped and consisted of an oblong block lying east and west, with a square tower containing a wheel-stair projecting externally from the centre of the south wall. While the plan of the northern portion of the main block is reminiscent of late 15th-century work the surviving portions of the early building are of a century later, having been built by Sir Patrick Hepburn in 1584. Sir Patrick's building has, in its turn, been extended and added to within modern times.

The masonry was of uncoursed rubble with freestone dressings, moulded and wrought with a quirked edge roll at the window jambs and ornamented with the cable and billet ornaments on the corbelling, which supported a turret projecting at eaves level from the south-west angle. A corresponding turret on the north-east and a turret-staircase within the east re-entering angle rested on moulded corbels without enrichment. The main block contained three storeys beneath the wall head and an attic within the roof.

The old entrance opened on the stair foot and passed through the south wall into a passage giving access to a chamber at either end, the northern being the kitchen; between these chambers were two smaller ones also entered off the passage.

An oak door, studded with bolts, taken from Kilspindie Castle was re-hung in the upper part of the staircase at Luffness.

Round the house are the relics of a considerable ditch and of regularly drawn mounds. These probably represent the camp raised by the French commander De Thermes in the summer of 1549 to block English

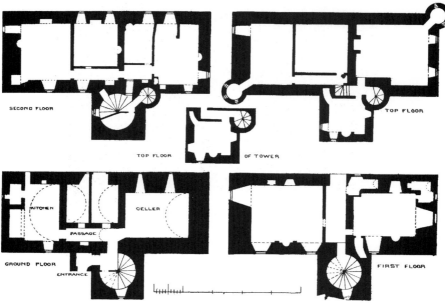

Luffness House – plans

supplies to their garrison at Haddington. In January 1552 the fort of Aberlady was ordered by the Queen-Regent and the lords to be delivered to Patrick Hepburn of Wauchton to be cast down and destroyed, "except the houses and mansioun thereof"; the artillery to be taken to Dunbar, the mansion and house to be enjoyed by Patrick and his heritage.

Brief History

In 1451 Robert de Bykkirtoune lord of Lufnois granted half the lands, but not the castle or head messuage, to Patrick Hepburn of Waughton, and in 1464 William de Bekirtoune, son and heir of Robert, with his father's consent, conveyed the remainder including the head messuage to the same Hepburn in exchange for lands elsewhere. David Hepburn of Waughton in 1498 transferred the barony of Waughton and that of Luffness to his son and heir Kentigern.

This is a private residence and should be viewed only from the highway.

Luffness House

15 Saltcoats Castle (*)

Ordnance Survey (OSR) = NT 486819

As you enter Gullane turn right on the East Links Road, and park before Waverley House. It is then a few hundred metres to the castle.

Structure

The remains of this castle are situated on a level site due south of Gullane. The ruin has at first sight the appearance of being considerably older than it really is, but analysis of the structure shows it to have been built towards the end of the 16th century. Erected on a courtyard plan, the main structure formed the southern boundary, and a range of subsidiary buildings has apparently run parallel to this on the north with the courtyard wall on east and west to complete the enclosure.

The portions now remaining are fragmentary; of the main buildings the north wall and the inner partitions are absent; of the buildings on the north only one portion at the north-east angle is complete and that only on the ground floor.

At a later period a segmental arch has bridged the interspace between the towers, as though the builder had decided to add to a domestic structure details of an earlier age.

In the north tower were gunloops: the lower cruciform, the upper keyhole-shaped; these appeared to have been more ornamental than useful.

The building was constructed of coursed rubble with ashlar dressings. It had been entered from the courtyard by a doorway, now only represented by its west jamb, in the north wall close to the tower at ground level. The ground floor contained three apartments ceiled with semi-circular barrel-vaults; the central one ran north and south, those at the ends east and west. These chambers had narrow slits on the south admitting little light.

Saltcoats Castle

A narrow turnpike staircase in the north tower gave access to the first floor level and there terminated. The first floor was lit by large windows in the south wall, of which the upper portions had been glazed, the lower closed by shutters.

Brief History

It remained entire until around 1810, and was inhabited till the end of the 18th century, when its last tenant Mrs Carmichael died there. At the beginning of the 18th century the estate was acquired by John Hamilton of Pencaitland who married Margaret Menzies, the heiress of Saltcoats.

Easily accessible on foot from Gullane.

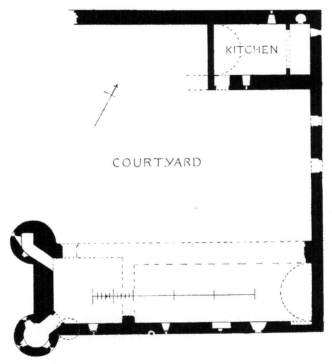

Saltcoats Castle – plan

16 Dirleton Castle (*)

Ordnance Survey (OSR) = NT 518840

Return to the A198 and travel for 2 miles. Turn left into Dirleton on B1345, and the castle is on the right. The Castle Inn, in Dirleton is well worth a visit.

Structure

This imposing ruin was built on the crest of an outcrop of rock. A dry ditch strengthens the southern face of the site, in which is set the main entrance. This was spanned by a bridge, probably of wood, supported on stone piers, which still remain in the ditch. Traces of a ditch are seen also at the north-eastern angle of the site. On the west the rock is sufficiently steep to make a further obstacle unnecessary. On the east, where the rock has an easy gradient, there is no trace of any outwork.

The three main periods may be traced in the castle buildings (13th, 15th and 16th centuries). In the 13th century the castle appears to have consisted of an enclosure formed by walls of enceinte following the perimeter of the site very much on the line of the walls now standing. The south-western angle contains the main building, which has towers, semi-circular and oblong, projecting outwardly. East of this the south wall is penetrated by the main entrance and originally terminated at the south-east angle in a circular tower, of which only the lower portion remains.

The existing ranges of building against the east and west curtains were erected in the 15th century, but these structures appear to incorporate older buildings, particularly at the south-eastern angle.

The 16th-century building comprises a structure now forming the northern boundary of a court at the south-west angle with adjoining towers containing the staircases.

The 13th-century masonry was of ashlar blocks built with a batter towards the base. The stone used was a fine-grained hard white sandstone and a similarly tinted but much softer stone resembling that from Gullane Quarry in the vicinity.

Dirleton Castle

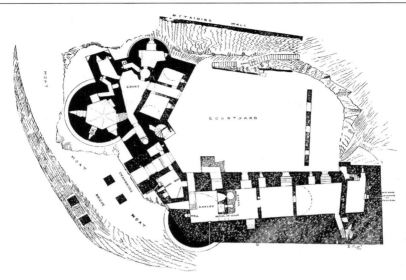

Dirleton Castle - plan

The principal building is the great drum tower on the south and contained, on the ground floor, an irregular hexagonal chamber, rib-vaulted, within walls about 10-feet thick.

The eastern end of the court had been vaulted over to form a pend at ground level; the stubs of the vault ribs were seen on the wall at either side.

The original mode of access to the upper floor is hard to determine. At this height the rooms in the southern towers intercommunicated by a mural passage, and the level is now reached by 16th-century wheel staircases. The remains of a fore-stair against the south wall of the court suggest that there was an entrance on the first floor over that portion of the pend, which has been destroyed.

The first floor of the great tower was once the principal apartment of the castle. It was similar in shape to the lower storey and had a lofty vaulted roof, from which the ribs have disappeared.

The curtain walls show entrances on the east, south and west. That in the south wall – the main entrance – appears to be a later construction probably of the 15th century.

The eastern range of buildings is mainly a 15th-century structure. The lowest storey formed a cellarage partially excavated from the rock and ceiled with a lofty barrel vault. The building and stair towers forming the north wall of the little court at the south-west angle were built circa 16th century.

Brief History

The family of De Vaux possessed the lands of Dirleton and Gullane about the middle of the 12th century. Their castle is specifically mentioned c. 1225. In the summer of 1298, when Edward I was lying at Kirkliston in Linlithgowshire, the Scots from Dirleton Castle, which the king had passed by on his march, were harassing his foraging parties. He therefore sent the Bishop of Durham to capture it, but his first attacks were a failure owing to a deficiency of siege machines and of food. On the receipt of fresh supplies a further attack on 14th and 15th July was successful, the garrison being allowed to go with their lives and property. In 1299 Robert de Maudlee was governor of Driltone for

Edward I, and in 1311 it was still in English hands. Within the first half of the 14th century the castle and lands passed by marriage to the family of Halyburton, and in 1389 Sir John Halyburton had a protection from Richard II for the castle and barony of Drylton.

While in ward in the king's hands in 1363, it was seized by William, Earl of Douglas, as the first step in a revolt against David II for misappropriation of public money. In 1505 James IV was at Dirleton. Early in the 16th century the Halyburton line in its turn ended in heiresses, of whom the eldest conveyed Dirleton to her husband's family, the Ruthvens, afterwards (1581) Earls of Gowrie.

In 1650 it was a nest of the moss-troopers who killed many soldiers of the army. Major-General Lambert and Colonel Monk with 1600 men came before the castle on November 7th and next morning opened fire from their batteries. The fourth shot killed the lieutenant of the moss-troopers and the garrison surrendered.

Administered by Historic Scotland. Open all year. Tel 01620 850330. Admission charge

Dirleton Castle

17 North Berwick Priory (*)

Ordnance Survey (OSR) = NT 546850

Continue on the secondary road and rejoin the A198 eastwards. Pass the railway station and turn right on Abbey Road. After approximately 200 yards is the Abbey Residential Home for Older People, adjoining which is the North Berwick Priory.

Structure

What survives of this foundation lies within the grounds of a modern residence. It consists of an oblong range of conventual buildings running east and west constructed of local rubble with yellow freestone dressings. The western portion has been storeys and an attic in height. The basement floor contained four cellars ceiled with semi-circular barrel vaults. In the east gable was a large pointed arched window or door, which opened into the upper floor of an oblong two-storeyed building in line with the western portion. Midway between these buildings there projects on the north a square tower built of ashlar, which is evidently an addition of the late 16th century. A circular turret is corbelled out at the north-eastern angle and is enriched by two string courses, the upper of which returns across the face of the square tower and, like the basement course, around a circular tower, built within the west re-entering angle which contained a fairly spacious circular stair leading to the upper floors of the west portion and square tower.

Brief History

This house for Cistercian nuns was founded probably in the third quarter of the 12th century. A papal bull of Clement VII, calendared in H.M Register House and dated 4th May 1525, confirmed to Isabella Hume the priory of North Berwick.

In 1548 Margaret, the prioress, and convent granted their principal estate at North Berwick to her brother Alexander Hume, brother of Patrick Hume of Polwarth. The perils to which the monastery was exposed were further illustrated by the formal restoration by Margaret on 14th May 1550, of valuables and vestments committed to her custody "in time of invasion by our old enemies of England".

The external structure is visible from public land, but access for photographs must be obtained from the residential home.

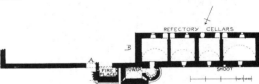

North Berwick Priory – plan

North Berwick Priory

18 Castle Tarbet

Ordnance Survey (OSR) = NT 513868

Fidra

The remains are on the island of Fidra, and therefore permission should be obtained from the RSPB and then enquire at the harbour about boat trips or hiring a boat.

Structure

It is the remains of a mortar built wall, which had probably formed a parapet.

Access: see above.

Fidra and Castle Tarbet

19 The Bass Castle (*)

Ordnance Survey (OSR) = NT 602873

> Enquire at the Scottish Seabird Centre (01620 890202), where they arrange regular trips to Bass Rock.

Structure

The remains are situated on Bass Rock in the estuary of the Forth. They are of the 16th century and are built in rubble of the trap rock of the site with mixture of imported light coloured freestone added in the dressings. Facing south-south-west is a great screen wall, from which a second wall, almost rectangular to it, returns in a southerly direction on the slope to the edge of the cliff. Parapets crenellated for guns surmount these walls. There is an entrance in the east screen wall within which is an enclosure before the gable of the residential portion. This latter is a structure of two storeys and a garret.

Brief History

In 1338 Alexander de Ramsay in a boat from the Bass ran the blockade of Dunbar Castle. In 1405 Prince James, on his way to France, went by boat from North Berwick to "the Castell of the Bas", where he waited for a ship from Leith and thence sailed to his capture off the Yorkshire coast.

In 1671 the Bass was purchased for the Crown, and the castle became a State prison, most of the occupants being Covenanters. The great event in the history of the fortress was when four Jacobite officers confined there in 1691 managed to surprise the place, got rid of the keepers and held the fortress for King James for nearly three years. In 1701 it was dismantled.

> Access: see above.

© Reproduced by kind permission of John Pringle

The Bass Castle

20 Fenton Tower (*)

Ordnance Survey (OSR) = NT 543822

Exit North Berwick southwards on the B1347 to Haddington. After 2 miles through Kingston, Fenton Tower is on your left.

Structure

The ruin of this tower, which dates from the 16th century, occupied a conspicuous position on the rising ground of Kingston Hill. The structure was built on an L-plan with the main block lying east and west and the short wing projecting southwards in alignment with the west gable. The main block contained three storeys and an attic floor, the latter lit by dormer windows. The lowest storey of this portion was occupied by the main staircase, which ascended only to the first floor. Above this level were three storeys, each of one apartment, reached from a turret staircase corbelled out in the re-entering angle. From the north wall of the main block a semi-circular tower projected and contained, between ground and first floor levels, a small circular staircase.

Ian Simpson and John Macaskill, decided to start the Tower's restoration in 1998. As it is a listed ancient monument and a Category A-listed building, Historic Scotland supervised the meticulous restoration. In 2002 its doors were once again open, and can be booked for a holiday.

Brief History

Patrick Whytelaw, son of Lord Ruthven, constructed the current building around 1550, a typical fortified tower of the time. In 1587, ownership was forfeited to Sir John Carmichael.

In 1591, a rebel army in Fife surrounded King James VI of Scotland, but fortunately the local townspeople rallied to his support and helped him escape. James took the ferry across the Firth of Forth to North Berwick and then took refuge with the Carmichaels at Fenton Tower.

Fenton Tower – today

James VI granted the Tower to Sir Thomas Erskine, who became Lord Dirleton, Viscount Fenton and later Earl of Kellie.

In 1631, the Tower passed to Sir John Maxwell of Innerwick, who became Earl of Dirleton in 1646. However his enjoyment was short-lived when in 1650 Oliver Cromwell invaded Scotland and he sacked Fenton Tower along with nearby Dirleton Castle.

The Tower can be seen from the road, but if you wish to receive details on accommodation then please telephone 01620 890089, or email manager@fentontower.com or visit the web site at www.fentontower.co.uk.

Fenton Tower – before restoration

21 Sydserf

Ordnance Survey (OSR) = NT 542818

From Fenton Tower continue on the B1347 for about 0.5 miles and the building is on the left.

Structure
Sydserf comprises a much-altered L-plan house; now of two storeys, probably dating from the 17th century. The basement is not vaulted, the roof has been altered and the house lowered, but there are two shot holes in one wall.

Can be seen from the roadside.

Sydserf

22 Waughton Castle (*)

Ordnance Survey (OSR) = NT 567809

> From Sydserf continue on the B1347. Turn left on minor road after Congalton Mains. After 1.25 miles Waughton Castle is on your right.

Structure

The south-west angle was occupied by the house, of which only a small projecting wing remains. This rises from the base of the rock and was built of the local igneous rubble with light coloured freestone dressings at quoins and voids. A narrow window in the south wall has an edge-roll with flanking hollows wrought on jambs and lintel, which suggests a 16th-century date for the structure.

On north and east a wall bound the rock, but this and the ruined structure at the north-east angle were much later than the house.

From the rock a staircase, only partially artificial, led down to the garden ground at base.

Brief History

On 14th January 1569 Waughton Castle was the scene of a raid by "Robert Hepburne, sonne to ye Waughtone and brake ye stabills and tooke out 16 horses: the laird of Carmichale being capitane and keeper of the said house of Waughtone."

> The ruins of the castle can be seen from the road.

Waughton Castle

23 Balgone House

Ordnance Survey (OSR) = NT 567825

Continue on the minor road, and turn left at the first opportunity, and first left again. Balgone House is just over 0.5 miles on the minor roads.

Structure

The long three-storey mansion incorporates an L-plan tower house of the early 17th century at the east end, which can be seen from the south-east angle of the range. The harled walls rise to three storeys and an attic, with crow-stepped gables.

Brief History

Ross of Hawkhead and the Semples were early owners of Balgone. In 1680 George Suttie, a merchant in Edinburgh, carried Balgone, and in 1702 he was created a baronet.

It is private property and privacy should be acknowledged.

Balgone House

24 Tantallon Castle (*)

Ordnance Survey (OSR) = NT 596851

Return to the minor road from Balgone, then turn left and second right. Follow the country lane through Blackdykes and Woodlea towards the A198. Turn right on the A198, and after 1.25 miles use the Historic Scotland car park and walk to the castle.

Structure

The buildings consist of a central gatehouse, from which extends to the north-west and east-north-east a great curtain wall terminating at either extremity of the site in circled towers. The ruins of a range of buildings occupy the northern side of the enclosure.

The front of the gatehouse has been greatly altered, and what remained was largely obscured by the great frontal addition built after 1528. In the original arrangement the entrance, protected by fosse, drawbridge and portcullis, lay within a framework formed by two rectangular piers salient to the curtain and surmounted by massive and lofty circular turrets joined by an arch at the present height of the curtain parapets. When raised the drawbridge fitted into the recess formed by piers and arch. The turrets probably terminated in embattled parapets and rose to three storeys.

Brief History

Tantallon came into notice with the rising fortunes of the Douglas family, who obtained the barony of North Berwick around 1371. In 1479, 24 years after the Douglas forfeiture, Archibald, 5th Earl of Angus received a grant of it from James III. The next Earl of Angus, after he had married the queen-mother of James V and lost influence over the person and councils of that young monarch, shut himself up in Tantallon, and defied for a time the whole hostile force of the kingdom. James raised the siege and only got possession because Angus fled to England. After James V's death, the earl obtained leave to return from his exile; in 1543 he was restored to his possessions, and began to make Tantallon stronger, and here he died in 1556. In 1639 the Covenanters garrisoned it against the king. About the beginning of the 18th century,

Tantallon Castle

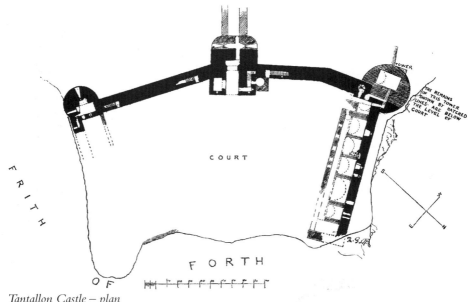

COURT

F R I T H

F O R T H

O F

THE REMAINS OF THIS TOWER SHOWN BY HATCHED LINES ARE THE LEVEL OF COURT BELOW

Tantallon Castle – plan

Sir Hew Dalrymple bought it from the Duke of Douglas, dismantled it and gave it up to decay.

The castle is in the care of Historic Scotland. Open April to Sept. daily, Oct to March Saturday-Wednesday. Tel: 01620 892727.

Tantallon Castle

25 Auldhame (*)

Ordnance Survey (OSR) = NT 714769

From Tantallon Castle continue on the A198 for 0.5 miles. On the z-bend at Auldhame, turn left off the main road to Seacliff Park, and park after 500 yards down the track. Auldhame is to the left among the trees overlooking a ridge.

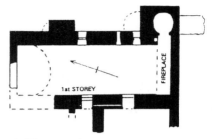

Auldhame – plan

Structure

The ruin, which is that of a large 16th-century mansion, consisted of a main block from north-north-west to south-south-east; from the eastern wall two rectangular towers projected eastwardly and circled turrets were corbelled out in the northern re-entrant angles. At the northern angles of the main block there appeared to have been circled turrets. It has been at least three storeys in height, a portion of the basement vaulted.

and Auldhame, son of a merchant burgess of Edinburgh, was King's Advocate in the reign of James V. In 1594 there was a charter of novodamus by James VI to Thomas Otterburn of Reidhall and Mariota Lauder his wife, of the lands of Auldhame in the barony of Tynningham.

Freely accessible.

Brief History

Auldhame belonged to the family of Otterburn; Sir Adam Otterburn of Reidhall

Auldhame

26 Seacliff Tower (*)

Ordnance Survey (OSR) = NT 613844

From Auldhame return to the A198 and the turn left to Scoughall. Then head for Seacliff and park. The ruin is along the coast.

Structure

A ruinous structure that probably dates from the end of the 16th century. It was oblong and at the western end there has been a small rectangular wing, probably a stair tower. The walls are reduced in places to the present ground level, and the north-west wall included a fireplace, slop drain and window. The building is known locally as "Sligo's Lookout". At least three storeys in height, a portion of the basement was vaulted.

Brief History

The property was apparently originally called Scougal and was held by the family of the same name.

Freely accessible.

Seacliff Tower

27 Whitekirk (*)

Ordnance Survey (OSR) = NT 595816

From Seacliff return to the A198 and the turn right and continue southwards. Whitekirk is on your right in the village.

Structure

Overlooking the church the long narrow structure was built of rubble with ashlar dressings, and originally it was the tithe barn of the village. It contained two storeys with a garret in the roof. The western portion is older than its adjunct and was the remains of a tower.

Three courses below the eaves on the south wall was a panel containing an angel figure supporting a shield. On the ground floor the western portion led to an unlit vaulted chamber; at the north end of the east wall a doorway led to a straight staircase within the thickness of the north wall and might also have led to the eastern portion of the structure.

Brief History

Built for himself, Oliver Sinclair, after 1540 out of the pilgrim's houses. The English in their invasion of Lothian in 1544 burned "A castle of Oliver Sanckler's". Later, during the English occupation of Haddington in 1548 they burnt "a village named the Longhoet Whyte Kirk belonging to 'Oliver Sainkle' and his own house where he lived."

It is a private property, but can be well seen from the road or from the kirkyard of the church – the attractive and historic church is open to the public.

Whitekirk

28 Tyninghame House

Ordnance Survey (OSR) = NT 619798

From Whitekirk continue on the A198 south for about 1.5 miles and the entrance to the house and gardens is on the left.

Structure

The house could have been of the 16th century and extended in 1617. Though a patchwork of pieces added by successive earls, it was so altered and enlarged about 1829 by William Burn, who re-faced the whole with native red sandstone, as to present the appearance of a large mansion, semi-Elizabethan, with small Scottish towers, and a beautiful terrace garden. The interior retained, with little alteration, its original form.

Private property and only open twice a year as part of the "Gardens of Scotland" scheme (www.gardensofscotland.org). Occasionally parties view the gardens by appointment.

Tyninghame House

29 Biel

Ordnance Survey (OSR) = NT 637759

From Tyninghame return to the A198 and turn left. Continue on the A198 for 1.25 miles; turn right onto the A1. Turn left to Stenton and left again to Newhall. Enter the gates to the estate.

Structure

At the eastern end of a castellated mansion is an early tower house, which had vaulted cellars possibly dating from the 13th century.

Brief History

The property was sold to John Hamilton, 1st Lord Belhaven in the mid 17th century and remained with the family until 1958, when it was sold to the current owner Charles Spence. The 2nd Lord Belhaven made a famous speech in the old Scottish parliament in 1706 against the Union of Parliaments. To that end there is a stone plaque on the house bearing the inscription in Latin "The first year of betrayal of Scotland".

Individual appointments are discouraged. Groups of 20 – 25 can be arranged with the proceeds going to charity. Tel: 01620 860355.

Biel

30 Belton House

Ordnance Survey (OSR) = NT 644766

From Biel, turn left and at the junction turn left to Dunbar. Keep left signed West Barns/Dunbar. Belton House is on your left. Keep on the B6370, and at the A1 turn right then left. Turn right on the A1087 to return to Dunbar.

Structure
The remains of a 16th-century tower house, which did have three barrel–vaulted chambers of the basement.

Brief History
The property was held by the Cunninghams of Belton, but passed by marriage in 1468 to the Hays of Yester. In 1687 it was granted to David Hay, second son of the Marquis of Tweeddale.

The ruins are in the grounds of a private residence. Please seek permission to view.

Belton House

31 Spott House

Ordnance Survey (OSR) = NT 679752

To respect the owner's wishes, this guide does not include any directions.

Brief History

Elias de Spot swore fealty to Edward I in 1296; and later the estate was held by the Humes, Douglases, Murrays and Hays. David Leslie spent the night before the Battle of Dunbar (1650) at Spott House, and from the top of Doon Hill he and his troops watched Cromwell below. In the annals of witchcraft this parish is famous as almost the last place in Scotland where reputed witches were burnt, as late as October 1705, on the top of Spott Loan.

It is a private residence.

Spott House

Castle Touring Guides

East Lothian (West)

Map 3 – East Lothian (West)

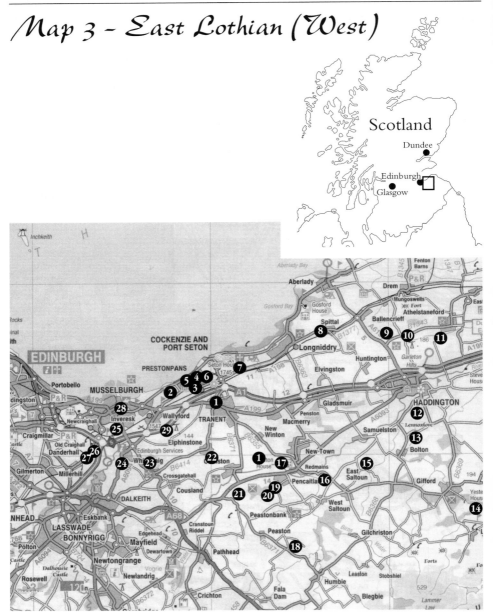

© Philip's 2003, © Crown copyright 2003

1 Tranent Tower (*)

Ordnance Survey (OSR) = NT 404729

Take the B6371/A198 from the A1 into Tranent. Go past the Tower Inn, and turn left on Sandersons Wynd. First left and left again into the cul-de-sac, where the tower is enclosed by a wall.

Structure

On plan it is L-shaped, the shorter limb being formed by a square tower, which projected southward from the south-west angle of the main block and housed a wheel-stair. It is three storeys in height, and only the basement is vaulted; the roof is covered with pantiles and the gables were crow stepped. The windows, which are unusually small, have chamfered jambs and lintels. The stair ascends from ground to the third floor, above which level the tower contained a dovecot with stone nests. The west room on the first floor had a large built up fireplace in the gable with aumbry recess adjoining and a stone sink with slop drain in the south wall. The tower dates from the 16th century.

Freely accessible to view from outside the wall.

Tranent Tower

2 Prestongrange House

Ordnance Survey (OSR) = NT 373737

From Tranent return towards the A1. Follow the signs over the A1 to Prestonpans (B1361), and turn right into the Musselburgh Golf Club.

Structure

Parts of the house date from the 16th century, but essentially it is a Scottish Baronial mansion, including a massive tower of 1830, and later. The two parts are linked with a corbelled stair-turret, which has a step-off, also corbelled, at the top.

Brief History

Robert de Quincy, Earl of Winchester, in 1184 bequeathed the estate to Newbattle Abbey and it was originally called Newbattle Grange. About the time of the Reformation c1560, the commendator and abbot, Mark Ker, had ownership, as well as the income of Prestongrange. He changed his religion and became a Protestant member of the Reformation Parliament, an Extraordinary Lord of Session and a Privy Councillor in 1569. After the death of the first Earl of Lothian in 1609; it was disposed of to John Morison, whose son, Sir Alexander Morison, Knt., as a Lord of Session, assumed the title of Lord Prestongrange (1626–31). So did the Lord Advocate, William Grant, who purchased the property in 1746, and whose second daughter married Sir George Suttie of Balgone.

It is the clubhouse, therefore written consent should be obtained from the Secretary. Tel 01875 810276 or web www.royalmusselburgh.co.uk.

Prestongrange House

3 Northfield House (*)

Ordnance Survey (OSR) = NT 389739

From Prestongrange House, return on the B1361 to Prestonpans. Turn left on the B1349 and Northfield House is on the right, just before the junction.

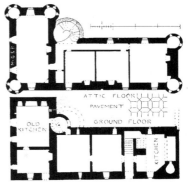

Northfield House – plan

Structure

George Hamilton built the mansion of the Marjoribanks of Northfield in 1590. It is two storeys, an attic and garret in height and is L-shaped on plan. The masonry is roughcast, but the freestone dressings were exposed; the roof was slated. The ground and first floor windows had backset margins; the attic and garret windows, the former constructed in stone the latter in timber, had simple triangular pediments. At attic floor level, circled turrets with conical slated roofs projected from the exterior angles and were borne on continuous corbelling.

The re-entering angle, lying to the north, contained a comparatively modern turret, within which was a geometrical stair; this turret probably replaced one earlier and smaller containing a wheel stair with a solid central newel. The eastward portion of the main wing had been altered very shortly after completion to contain the scale and platt stair and the south entrance.

The features include important early 17th-century painted ceilings, which are in excellent condition. There is Baltic pine flooring, original heavy studded wooden doors, slit windows and corbelled turrets on east and west elevations. There are two

Northfield House

kitchens, but the original one has a vaulted ceiling and a wide fireplace with a decorative over-mantel. The vestibule has a mosaic tile floor with a thistle motif, while the drawing room has turret rooms on three of its corners with a large open fireplace. The long inner hallway was once part of the great hall but it was partitioned off with the dining room in 1720.

Brief History

Joseph Marjoribanks, an Edinburgh merchant, acquired lands and houses on the south side of the village of salt-Preston, from George Hamilton portioner of Salt-Preston in 1609, and whose coat of arms adorns the main entrance. Marjoribanks and his wife, Marion Simpson, whose initials and the date 1611 grace the garden doorway, were probably responsible for a major re-modelling

and expansion of the existing mansion in the early 17th century. Soon after 1703, the house was sold to the Symes, an Edinburgh legal family, who subdivided the old great hall into more fashionable panelled rooms and plastered over the brightly painted ceilings. In 1896 the house passed to a mining engineer, James McNeil. His daughter sold the house to Schomberg Scott in 1953, and the current owner bought Northfield from Scott's executors in 1999.

It is a private residence and not open to the public. The gardens are normally open only on "Doors Open Day" which is usually towards the end of September. However the house is on the main street and is clearly visible.

Northfield House

4 Hamilton House (*)

Ordnance Survey (OSR) = NT 389739

At the junction beyond Northfield House, Hamilton House is on the left.

Structure

There is a main rectangular block running north and south with rectangular wings projecting westward from either end, all portions being two storeys in height. At the south re-entering angle a semi-hexagonal projection houses the staircase and the former entrance. Throughout the building is of freestone rubble and has been harled. The windows to north, east and south have chamfered jambs and lintels; the upper floor windows are dormers and have triangular pediments and raking cornices surmounted by a cinque-foliated finial, the cinquefoil being the Hamilton charge. On the south elevation the dormer pediments are elaborated and have horizontal cornices; the western pediment has a scrolled cartouche bearing a shield charged with three cinquefoils two and one for Hamilton and flanked by the initials I H for John Hamilton. The middle pediment bears the date 1628 flanking the monogram I H K S for John Hamilton and Katherine Simpson, his wife. Adjoining the south wing is a former entrance to the courtyard by a doorway with segmental head and roll-and-hollow mouldings of late Gothic detail.

Freely accessible for external viewing from the road.

Hamilton House

5 Preston Tower (*)

Ordnance Survey (OSR) = NT 393742

Take the next left turn after Hamilton House, and then first left with Preston Tower on the left.

Structure

The body of the building contained six storeys, while the jamb contained seven. The upper storeys within a parapet walk, which returned round the building except at the north wall of the shorter wing, were an addition of the early 17th century, built in a lighter coloured stone and exhibited Renaissance mouldings on the jambs and entablatures of the windows.

The parapet and angle rounds were contemporary with the upper storeys, but the corbelling appears to be earlier and might date from the 16th century. The windows, where unaltered, have a small chamfer worked on the jambs; the later windows had moulded jambs or backset margins or both.

The entrances to the tower were in the east wall and not within the re-entering angle. A great corbel, at the level of the parapet corbels, and a vestige of a neighbour show where a machiolated projection served those as a defence. The basement was entered through a round-headed doorway, which had two doors, the outer of timber, the inner an iron yet. Above the lower entrance, but nearer the south-east angle, there was a second, from which the hall was reached.

Brief History

The castle was burned by the Earl of Hertford in 1544, by Cromwell in 1650, and by accident in 1663, and was then abandoned. Sir William Hamilton (1791-1856), the learned Professor of Logic, re-acquired the ruined tower in the early part of the 19th century. Robert, brother of Sir William, led the Presbyterians in the actions of Drumclog and Bothwell Bridge.

Gardens open all year. Tower can only be viewed from the exterior.

Preston Tower – plans and section

Preston Tower

6 Harlawhill

Ordnance Survey (OSR) = NT 390745

From Preston Tower, go back 50 yards to the road, turn left and left again on East Loan. Follow the road for about 200 yards and the house is on the right just after a gentle z-bend.

Structure

This is a mid 17th-century L-plan house of two storeys with an ogee-roofed tower added later. Also to the east an 18th-century wing with scrolled skewputts.

The house is visible from the main road.

Harlawhill

7 Seton Palace

Ordnance Survey (OSR) = NT 418751

Seton Palace – coat of arms

From Harlawhill, return to the junction beyond the Preston Tower entry road. Turn left and then turn left on the B1361. Go straight over the roundabout on the A198 to North Berwick. After 0.75 miles the entrance drive for Seton House can be seen on the left, followed almost immediately by the entrance to the car park for Seton Collegiate Church. Park there and walk back to the Seton House drive where a corner tower from the outer wall of Seton Palace stands on the east side of the entrance to the drive; the remains of a sundial are mounted on the south wallhead. Return to the car park and follow the path to Seton Collegiate Church where there is a display of heraldic panels and pediments from the Palace. This is a Historic Scotland building so please check opening times.

Structure

The original plan was based around a triangular (actually a quadrangle) courtyard. "The house consisted of two large fronts of freestone, and in the middle is a triangular court. The front to the south east hath a very noble apartment of a Hall, a Drawing Room, a handsome Parlour, Bedchamber, Dressing Room and closet. This apartment seems to have been built in the reign of Mary, Queen of Scots; for on the ceiling of the great hall are plastered the Arms of Scotland, with the

Seton Palace – from an old drawing

Arms of France on one hand … the front to the North seems to be a much older building than this. The apartments of the state are on the second story, and very spacious; three great rooms, at least forty feet high, which they say were finely furnished, ever since Mary Queen of Scots, on her return from France, kept her apartments there."

The illustrations of the old palace were made in 1790 just prior to it's being demolished by the York Buildings Co. to make way for the more modern Seton Castle. There is little evidence of the old palace except for remnants of the mill, the collegiate church and the original garden walls. The south-western turret still stands as a reminder of the previous occupants of Seton Palace, the Earls of Winton.

lands named after the family since before the time David I. The lands of Seton took their name from the estates which were formally held in England; principally Seaton-Staithes, Yorkshire. The old Palace of Seton had endured much destruction and rebuilding over the centuries, being much destroyed because of its proximity to the main invasion route from England. It had, however, kept its original layout and French styling throughout its existence.

Can be viewed from the highway. Seton Collegiate Church open April-September. Tel 01875 813334.

Brief History
The Seton family's chief residence was at the splendid Palace of Seton. It had stood on the

Seton Palace

8 Redhouse Castle (*)

Ordnance Survey (OSR) = NT 463770

From Seton Palace, exit the car park and turn left along the A198 to Longniddry. After 2 miles on the eastern outskirts of Longniddry, take the second exit off the roundabout, signposted B1377 to Drem. In 1.25 miles Redhouse Castle is on the right, adjacent to the market gardens.

Structure

The house formed the northern side of a quadrangular courtyard that was bounded on the east by a range of outbuilding and on the south and west by boundary walls.

The courtyard was entered from the south through a wide gateway with a semi-circular head round which returned a roll-and-hollow moulding that continued down the jambs; the detail of the moulding indicated that the wall, which was built of rubble, was harled. Over the gateway five projecting corbels suggested that the entrance was surmounted by a little gatehouse, which projected outwardly on the corbels and was borne on the sturdy segmental

scoinson arch. The eastern outbuildings consisted of a range of vaulted cellars with, formerly, an upper storey within a very steeply pitched roof. Around the south, east and west walls an unmoulded stringcourse and a cavetto moulded eaves course return; the gables were stepped. The doorway in the west wall of the courtyard, and that of the cellarage of the east range, had good Scottish renaissance moulded architraves circa 17th century.

The south front is four storeys to the wall-head, above which was an attic lit by dormer windows, but the walls at the south-east angle were carried higher, providing apartments over the wheel-stair. The north front was more richly treated; a moulded stringcourse returned at the level of the turret upper corbel courses and a second at attic floor level. The corbelling of the north-west turret had numerous and delicate members, while that of the others was simple and massive, yet the turrets had undoubtedly been built at the same time.

Brief History

The lands of "Eister Spittell" or "Eister Reidspittell" or Redhouse came to John

Redhouse Castle

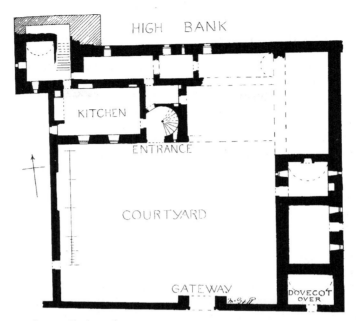

HIGH BANK

KITCHEN

ENTRANCE

COURTYARD

GATEWAY

DOVECOT
OVER

Redhouse Castle – plan

Laing, keeper of the royal signet and Rebecca Dennistoun his spouse, by purchase from the superior David Lindsay of Balcarres at the instigation and with the consent of Sir George Douglas of Redhouse and his heir; the royal confirmation to the charter is dated 1607. In 1612 there was a ratification of an instrument of sasine granted in 1608 by the late John Laing of "Spittellis" conferring the property on Sir Andrew Hamilton of Redhouse and Lady Jeanne Layng his wife, daughter and heiress of John Laing Hamilton being a judge or "senator of the Supreme Court". In 1621 a charter of novodamus of the lands of Easter Spittal with the manor erected the whole estate into the free barony of Reidhouse.

The ruin is close to the main road and is freely visible. The owner is a member of the Scottish Castles Association, and the Events Programme may include Redhouse Castle from time to time .

9 Byres

Ordnance Survey (OSR) = NT 495770

From Redhouse Castle, continue on the B1377 to the roundabout. Turn right on the A6137, and after 0.75 miles turn left to Byres Farm. Do not drive beyond the cottages, where an enquiry at the last cottage should be made for permission to enter the field.

Structure

It consists of the remains of a tower house or keep, rising to two storeys with a vaulted basement.

Brief History

It was originally a property of the Byres family, but passed to the Lindsays of the Byres. Patrick Lindsay, 6th Lord Lindsay of Byres, supported the Reformation, and was involved in the plot to murder Rizzio. He took a leading part in compelling Mary, Queen of Scots, to abdicate, and was a party in the Ruthven Raid. John Lindsay, 10th Lord Lindsay of Byres, was made Earl of Lindsay in 1633. He joined the Covenanters, and fought at Marston Moor in 1644 against Charles I.

Access: see above.

Byres

10 Garleton Castle (*)

Ordnance Survey (OSR) = NT 509767

From Byres return to the main road, and then turn left. Take the next left on the B1343 to Athelstaneford. Turn right at the junction, and then left. Garleton Castle is on the right. If you want a better view there is a short road on the southern side of the ruin.

Structure

The castle comprised an oblong enclosure containing a house with a jamb or small wing at the north-east corner and two little lodges set at the western ends of the north and south boundary walls. The house was at least three storeys in height.

Of the house there remain only the north and east lateral walls with indications of the west gable and interior partitions. In the basement were three vaulted cellars within the main block, that the western was the kitchen and that the oncome of the fireplace vent could still be traced. The staircase seemed to have been a turnpike built within the east wall. A forestair built external to the enclosure at the north-east angle, is secondary. The masonry is irregularly coursed rubble with dressings at voids.

The south-west lodge is oblong on plan and was two storeys in height; the upper floor reached from a forestair on the north, which appeared to have superseded an internal circular staircase contained within a projecting turret on the south. The ground floor contained two vaulted chambers, which originally communicated with each other.

Brief History

Apparently this was the successor of the house with lands of Easter Garleton or Garmylton owned by Sir John Towers of Inverleith, from whom the 3rd Earl of Winton bought half of Athelstaneford, conferring Garleton upon his 4th son, Sir John Seton, Bart., of Garleton, originator of that branch of the Seton family.

Freely visible from the road.

Garleton Castle

11 Barnes Castle (*)

Ordnance Survey (OSR) = NT 529766

Continue on the road from Garleton, and Barnes can be seen on the right on the ridge opposite Kilduff on the skyline. Turn right on the left bend in Athelstaneford, signposted East Linton (A1). At the junction turn right on the B1347, and then right again on the old A1. Turn right at the second turning signposted to Barney Mains. Park and take the 0.5 miles walk to the ruins.

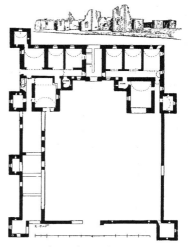

Barnes Castle – plan

Structure

This 16th-century building was never completed and is quite ruinous. On plan the structure is a great rectangle, with the major axis lying north-east and south-west. Square towers projected externally from the angles, and between these were spaced intermediate towers, two on the north-west, one on the south-east and one centrally on the south-west.

The dwelling was to have occupied the north-eastern part on the enclosure, and against the north-western wall were traces of a long range of building. The structure was built of rubble with freestone dressings.

Brief History

The connection of the Barnes estate with the Seton family began with the grant by Robert Bruce in 1321-2 to Alexander de Seyton of the whole land near Haddington called "the Bernis". In the person of John, 2nd surviving son of George, 7th Lord Seton, and the property was conferred on a cadet branch of the family. John served in Spain and returned to hold office in the household of James VI. John Seton of Barnes died in 1594.

Freely accessible.

Barnes Castle

12 Lennoxlove (*)

Ordnance Survey (OSR) = NT 515721

Return to the old A1 and turn right. At the double roundabout follow the signs to Haddington and Lennoxlove. On entering the town keep left avoiding the town centre. Taking the B6368 to Gifford, passing the Tynedale Tavern, take the left turn to Lennoxlove. Entry is 500 yards on the right.

Structure

It is an extensive and composite structure, manifestly the production of several building operations, the nucleus being the south-west portion, which is a 15th-century tower.

The tower is massive, L-shaped on plan and was once enclosed by a barmkin, but the only remaining portion of this was the entrance which lies to the north of the tower. It was a wide 16th-century gateway with a semi-circular head having a quirked cavetto moulding returning round the head and down the jambs. The tower is built of rubble and had been harled. The windows had evidently been enlarged and had a quirked edge-roll wrought on jambs and lintel. There were three main floors beneath and an attic floor above the parapet walk, which latter appeared to have been reconstructed circa late 16th century. The parapet was without embrasures, had open circular projections at all angles except the south-western, where there was a large cap house, and was borne on a continuous corbel course. It consisted of two members, of which the upper bore the billet enrichment and the lower was cabled. A Latin inscription over the massive north door of grated iron records that John Maitland, Earl of Lauderdale, improved this tower in 1626. The house today has pink sand-coloured stone additions of the 19th and early 20th century.

Brief History

It was originally called Lethington and belonged to the Maitland family. John Maitland (1616-82) was made Duke of Lauderdale, and it was used by him and other members of the family. When he died the property passed to his stepson, Lord Huntingtower, who owned other properties

Lennoxlove

and decided to sell it. The trustees of Frances Theresa Stewart, Duchess of Lennox and Richmond, purchased it. A grand daughter of the 1st Lord Blantyre, Francis Stewart was brought up in France at the court of the exiled Queen Henrietta Maria, wife of Charles I. By the time she was 15, Frances was already famous for her beauty. She was installed at the court of the newly restored Charles II where she caught the king's eye. He offered her gifts and titles, and he even made enquiries as to how he could best divorce his wife and marry Frances instead. However, she eloped with his cousin, Charles Gordon-Lennox, Duke of Richmond and Gordon, who died only five years later. They had no children so the Duchess left £50,000 for the purchase of a house for her nephew, Alexander Stewart, Master of Blantyre, on condition that it be called "Lennox's Love to Blantyre". In time the name was shortened to Lennoxlove. The House remained in the ownership of the Blantyre Stewarts for almost two centuries until 1900 when the 12th Lord Blantyre died without a male heir. The house passed to his second daughter Ellen. Her son, Major William Baird, began the work of restoration with Sir Robert Lorimer.

In 1946 the 14th Duke of Hamilton bought Lennoxlove.

It now incorporates the Nigel Tranter Centre, who was the first President of The Scottish Castles Association, which supported the development of the centre. Open Easter–October, Wed, Thu and Sun, 13.30–16.30; check if house is open on Sat before setting out. Tel 01620 823720 and web www.lennoxlove.org.

Lennoxlove

13 *Colstoun House*

Ordnance Survey (OSR) = NT 514712

> Return to the B6368 and turn left. In 1 mile turn left and the stone gate pillars into the grounds are on the right.

Structure

An old pele tower dating from the 12th century; virtually all subsumed within later extensions.

Brief History

It was a property of the Brown family from the 13th century or earlier. The Colstoun Pear was a magic pear given by Hugh of Yester or Gifford, a reputed wizard, to his daughter on her marriage to a Brown of Colstoun in the 13th century. So long as her family held and preserved the pear they would prosper. The pear, shrivelled to the size of a plum, is still kept at the house.

Sir William Brown of Colstoun defeated the English in a battle at Swordwellrig, Annandale, in the 15th century, at which Sir Marmaduke Langdale and Lord Crosby were slain.

> It is private residence and not open to the public, and this also applies to the grounds surrounding the property. Permission should be sought from the owners before entering.

Colstoun House

14 Yester Castle (*)

Ordnance Survey (OSR) = NT 556667

Continue on this minor road, and then turn right at the junction on the B6369 to Gifford and Garvald. Through Gifford take the left turn to Long Yester/Castle Park Golf Course. (The Tweeddale Arms Hotel in Gifford is ideal for a snack or an evening meal.) Turn left after 1.5 miles to Danskine and then pass the entrance to the golf course. Turn left to Castlemain Farm, and right at the row of cottages, where you should seek advice on the way to the ruins.

Yester Castle

Structure

It is built on a promontory, which lies north and south and is slightly crescentic in shape, with precipitous sides bounded by the waters.

The walls are for the most part levelled to the ground except on the north and east sides, where portions still stand to a height of forty feet. In other directions they have fallen. The masonry is built of reddish freestone ashlar set in large courses. At the base of these walls a heavy offset course with a weathered top

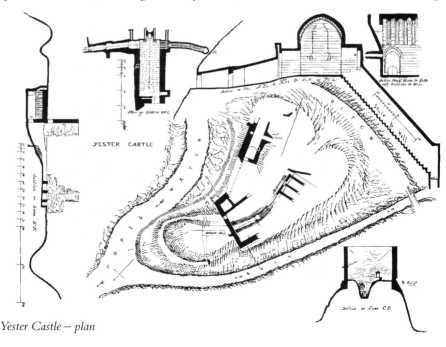

Yester Castle – plan

returned exteriorly. In the northern wall, at the level of the enceinte, an arched doorway, which had been closed by double doors, gave access to the northern portion of the site.

Brief History

The manor of Yester was granted by William the Lyon (1166-1214) to Hugh Gifford, whose father, an Englishman, had settled in Lothian under David I. Sir David Dalrymple related that his grandson, Hugh Gifford de Yester, died in 1267, and that in Yester Castle "there was a spacious cavern formed by magical art, and called in country Bo'Hall (Hobgoblin Hall)." Tradition reports that the castle was the last fortification which surrendered to the English general, sent into Scotland by the Protector Somerset

On February 24th 1548, Lord Grey of Wilton got possession of it and committed its guarding to Sir George Douglas with fifty men. By the end of April, however, Lord Grey reports it as kept by Spaniards and holding out against the English fort at Haddington, so that the Scottish-French forces must have recaptured it.

See above.

Yester Castle

15 Pilmuir House (*)

Ordnance Survey (OSR) = NT 486695

From Yester Castle return to the road out of Gifford and turn left on the B6355. After 2 miles take the first turn right after the B6368. The second right turn leads to Pilmuir but it is surrounded by a high wall.

Structure

The structure, two storeys and an attic and garret in height, was built on a simple plan, consisting of a main block running east-north-east and west-south-west and a smaller wing projecting on the north, which housed a spacious spiral staircase with a bedroom overhead. The exterior was unpretentious, having walls of rubble coated with a rough east, yet the crow-stepped gables and dormer pediments, the steeply pitched roof and the turret stair corbelled out over the west re-entering angle, gave individuality and character to the building.

The original entrance was in the projecting wing and communicated immediately through the stair well with the basement chambers.

The turret stair contained within the west re-entering angle led from the attic to the garret storey and was borne on the usual corbelling, but a squinch arch supported this, in its turn.

Brief History

William Cairns of Pilmuir, who died in 1653, had a son Richard, who succeeded him, but dying left the estate entailed upon William Borthwick eldest son of his sister Sibilla and Alexander Borthwick in Johnstounburn. The deed of entail is dated 1659. William Borthwick was dead before 1689.

It is a private property and not visible from the road.

Pilmuir House

16 Saltoun Hall

Ordnance Survey (OSR) = NT 461685

From Pilmuir, continue on the minor road before the last turn, and keep left until you return to the B6355. At the junction turn right and after 0.5 miles it is a right turn into Saltoun Hall.

Structure

It is a large and imposing mansion in the Tudor style, but there is an earlier nucleus overlaid and obscured by the modern work, and this goes back at least as far as the early 17th century. This portion is the part on the west, which crests the steep river bank. It is now four storeys in height and has been refaced, but the basement still retains stone-vaulted ceilings.

Brief History

In the 12th and the first half of the 13th century the manor of Salton belonged to the De Morvilles, Lords High Constables of Scotland, and their successors, the Lords of Galloway; but about 1260 the greater part of it seems to have been possessed by Sir William de Abernethy, whose descendant, Laurence, was created Baron Saltoun in 1445. In 1643 the 9th Lord Saltoun sold the estate to Sir Andrew Fletcher, a judge-of-session, with the title of Lord Innerpeffer, among whose descendants were Andrew Fletcher (1653–1716), the patriot and political writer.

It is privately occupied as separate dwellings and permission should be sought before entering the grounds.

© Reproduced by kind permission of John Pringle

Saltoun Hall

17 Winton House

Ordnance Survey (OSR) = NT 439696

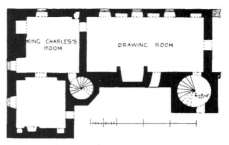

Continue on the B6355 and then turn left into Pencaitland. The entrance into Winton House is signposted on the right.

Structure

Today there is no trace of the Seton's first castle at Winton. The oldest surviving remains, a strong vaulted kitchen, date back to the 15th century. When Lord Seton built that tower house is not known, although George, created the 1st Lord Seton in 1451, is traditionally given the credit.

The present building is a striking architectural structure, and though following the Tudor style in its stacks of columned chimneys and in the decorative architraves of its windows, is quite distinguishable from that era. Additions made about 1805 in the English Baronial style were destroyed by fire in May 1881.

What remains of the earliest masonry is of freestone rubble.

Winton House – plan

Brief History

Robert, 6th Lord Seton, managed to stand high in James VI's favour despite his being a Roman Catholic. He frequently entertained the king and queen at his principal seat, Seton Palace. In return, he was created 1st Earl of Winton in November 1600. The newly ennobled earl set about rebuilding his residence at Winton, badly damaged by the English in 1544. Following his death in 1603, his second son, George, who became 3rd Earl of Winton, pressed on with the scheme and, between 1620 and 1627, employed William Wallace, the King's Master Mason, to oversee the operation.

The Winton estates, forfeited by the 5th Earl

Winton House

of Winton in 1716, were sold to the York Buildings Company, and on its failure part of the property, including Winton Castle, was acquired by James Hamilton, Lord Pencaitland, whose great-great-granddaughter, Mary Campbell, in 1813 married James, 6th Lord Ruthven (1777–1853), and died in 1885.

The house is open on the first weekends of April, May, August and September between 12.30 and 16.30. The telephone number is 01875 340222 or web www.wintonhouse.co.uk.

Winton House

18 Keith Marischal (*)

Ordnance Survey (OSR) = NT 449643

Through Pencaitland take the first left over the bridge. At the junction go straight across (Glenkinchie Distillery to the right), and then turn right at the next junction. After 1.5 miles turn left to Keith Marischal, and then first left. The tower house is on the right after 1 mile.

Structure

The structure dates from the late 16th century, but during the 18th century it was repaired in the Gothic style. Into the north wall of the north-west wing was built a stone bearing beneath an earl's coronet a shiel charged with three pallets on a chief – the arms of the Keith family.

Near the angle turret, but towards the west, a panel has been inserted. It bears the arms of Sir George Skene of Rubislaw and Fintry and is dated 1688; and was removed from Rubislaw to the west of Aberdeen.

Brief History

Originally known as Keith House, it was once the seat of the Earls Marischal before passing to the Earl of Hopetoun. The timber used in its construction was a gift from the King of Denmark, to George, 5th Earl, in 1589, after he went thither to conduct to Scotland Princess Anne, who was betrothed to James VI. George died at Dunnottar in 1623.

It is a private property, but it can be partially seen from the road.

© Crown Copyright: RCAHMS

Keith Marischal

19 Woodhall

Ordnance Survey (OSR) = NT 433680

Return to the main road and turn left to Peaston, and then right at the junction, on the B6371. After 1.5 miles turn right, signposted Templehall, and then left to Pencaitland. At the right hand bend Woodhall is on the private road to the left.

Structure

The dwelling house of Woodhall incorporated a portion of a small tower of the 16th century that was restored in 1884. The original portion was a two-storeyed structure built of yellow freestone rubble originally covered with roughcast. At the north-east angle a circled turret was corbelled out. The basement chamber is vaulted.

Brief History

Early in the 17th century Woodhall was in the possession of John Sinclair of Herdmanston, but in 1644 confirmation was given of a charter in which Sinclair resigned the barony of Wester Pencaitland, including Woodhall and its manor-place, in favour of Robert Sinclair of Longformacus (Berwickshire), and the place was still in the ownership of that family at the end of the century.

Woodhall is on a private road, so it is advisable to write for permission.

Woodhall

20 Penkaet Castle

Ordnance Survey (OSR) = NT 427677

Continue after Woodhall and Penkaet Castle is a further 600 yards on the road.

Structure

The building sits close to the ground and comprised a long central block, with main axis lying north-east and south-west, two storeys and an attic in height; at either end a wing projected southwards, the eastern being the longer, narrower and lower. The wing on the west was three storeys and an attic in height and, with the western central block, comprised the earliest portion; it may date from the later years of the 16th century, while the east wing, which is dated 1638, is later but, as the detail throughout is identical and of the type between 1625 and 1650, the building may be described as though it was entirely of this one period.

The building is of light coloured freestone rubble covered with harling except at the dressings, which are exposed. The windows had dressed and backset margins chamfered at jams and lintel. The dormer windows had moulded horizontal and raking cornices enclosing triangular pediments, which were surmounted by decayed finials trefoiled or crescented.

Brief History

Sir John Lauder, who in 1688 was created a baronet of Nova Scotia, and whose ancestors had been lairds of the Bass Rock from the 13th to the 16th century, acquired the lands of Fountainhall. The lands comprised Easter and Wester Templehall to the south, Huntland to the east and Dryburgh lands, and had previously belonged to a family of Pringle of Woodhead or Southwood. The king granted to Robert Pringle, Writer to the Signet, his wife, Violet Cant and John Pringle his son and heir these lands in 1636, including Southwood alias Woodhead, after resignation by George Cockburn of Ormiston. Robert Pringle was the builder of the present house. He was succeeded in Woodhead (as it was then known) by John Pringle and another John before the whole property was disposed of to Lauder and its name changed. In 1689 Sir John Lauder was raised to the bench as Lord Fountainhall, known for his historical and legal collections. The Lauders of Fountainhall were connected, by rather remote descent, with the Lauders of the Bass, and bore the white griffin of that family on their registered arms.

Private property.

Penkaet Castle

21 Ormiston Castle

Ordnance Survey (OSR) = NT 413677

> Return to the B6371, and turn right. In 0.75 miles turn right by the lodge and the house, which incorporates older work, is 200 yards on the right.

Brief History

The property originally belonged to the Lindsays, but passed to the Cockburns in the 14th century. In 1545 George Wishart, the protestant martyr, was taken from Ormiston to Cardinal Beaton, who had him burned to death at St Andrews. The castle was occupied by the English in 1547 as Cockburn of Ormiston sided with them. The Earl of Arran retook Ormiston, burned it and even cut down the trees around it as revenge for Cockburn's treachery. In 1748 it was sold to the Hope Earl of Hopetoun.

> Exterior visible from the road

Ormiston Castle

22 Elphinstone Tower

Ordnance Survey (OSR) = NT 391698

Return to the B6371 and turn right, and then right at the junction on the A6093. Turn left on the B6371 through Ormiston, and left again towards the Elphinstone Research Centre. Turn left at the junction to Elphinstone. Through the village the tower is signposted on the left.

Structure

At the end of the 19th century it was still a square three-storeyed pile and well preserved. The two lower storeys retained their stone vaulting and the uppermost having been re-roofed with slate. It is now less than one storey, oblong on plan, from the original three main storeys beneath the wall-head, which terminated in a parapet walk with rudimentary corner rounds, all borne on moulded corbels with moulded interspaces of late 16th-century design. The walls were of coursed ashlar with long and short quoins.

Elphinstone Tower – c. 1890

At ground level a basement course with a splayed set-off returns and was stopped on either side of the entrance doorway, which was set in the north wall a little above the ground. This doorway had a segmental head and its giblet checked to receive an outer timber door, which opened outwards, and an inner grate of iron opening inwardly. The windows had splayed jambs and lintels and

Elphinstone Tower – today

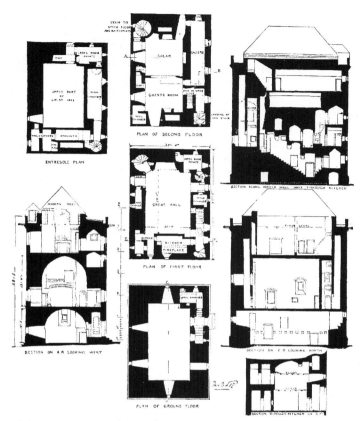

Elphinstone Tower – plans and sections

had been heavily barred and stanchioned. At the north-east angle could be traced the outline of a much later building, which communicated with the lower floors of the tower. A 17th-century heraldic panel, removed from the original building, can still be seen on the south wall of the existing farmhouse.

In the 1960s the tower was partially dismantled for safety reasons and little now survives.

Brief History

The tower was probably erected in the 15th century, when Sir Gilbert Johnstone, son of Sir Adam of Johnstone, came into possession of the property by marriage with Agnes Elphinstone, the heiress. Andrew Johnstone of Elphinstone is on record in 1551. The line ended with Sir James, 3rd baron Elphinstone, who was alive in 1673, but had to part with the estates and whose fate is unknown.

In December 1545 George Wishart was brought from Ormiston to Elphinstone Tower by the Earl of Bothwell and handed over to Cardinal Beaton. Wishart was then taken to St Andrews for trial as a heretic and was burned at the stake.

The ruined tower is in the garden of a private house, and contact should be made with the owner to view.

23 Carberry Tower

Ordnance Survey (OSR) = NT 364697

> Continue on the A6414 to the traffic lights. Turn right on the A6124 and pass Carberry Candles: the entrance to Carberry Tower is a further 300 yards on the right.

Structure

Carberry Tower is an old house, some say dating from 1480. Certainly the oldest part existed by the early 16th century. The tower forms the north-west angle of the mansion which has grown around it in the course of time, oblong on plan, with modern extensions, leaving only the north and west faces of the tower unobscured. In height there are two main storeys, both vaulted, but beneath each vault there had been an entresol with timber floor. The wall-head was surmounted by a massive parapet, which had large merlons, finishing in a large weathered cope. The parapet slightly overhangs and was borne on a continuous corbelling, a cavetto in section, enriched with winged heads. The roof within the parapet was flat and may have been intended as a gun-platform; the merlons, or solids, were unusually massive and had heavy sloping copes, while the central merlon on each side except the southern is pierced by a gun-loop.

The masonry of the parapet is inferior to that of the lower part of the walls and may be secondary. The turret at the south-west angle is modern. The lower part of the walls was constructed in rubble.

Brief History

"Caerbairin" is the earliest reference to Carberry, in connection with some lands belonging to the Crown in the 11th century – later granted to the monks of Dunfermline by David I.

When Sir Alexander Elphinstone was killed in 1435 at the battle of Piperdean, his daughter married a Johnstone and the Tower went with her. To this Tower the reformer Wishart was taken in 1546 and brought before Cardinal Beaton before being burnt at the stake.

It may have been James Riggs who built the new house in 1598, and the Riggs occupied Carberry until 1668. The Commissioner Sir Adam Blair of Lochwood bought the estate, but his tenure was taken away from him in 1689 as a result of the Glorious Revolution.

> It is a residential Christian conference centre, offers accommodation, and viewing should be by appointment. Tel 0131 665 3135 or web www.carberrytower.com

Carberry Tower

24 Smeaton Castle

Ordnance Survey (OSR) = NT 347699

Continue on the A6124 and at the roundabout turn left on the A6094 through Whitecross, and stay on the A6094, where the tower is on the right.

Structure

It consists of a much-altered 15th-century courtyard castle, with round corner towers, only two of which remain. One range of buildings survives, as does the curtain wall between the two towers, but little remains of the rest of the castle, except traces of a ditch. One round tower, rising to four storeys, has an adjoining square stair-tower, while the other tower has been reduced in height. The walls have been pierced by gunloops.

The ruined tower is now part of a farm, and permission should be sought for a closer inspection.

Smeaton Castle

25 Inveresk Lodge

Ordnance Survey (OSR) = NT 348716

Return through Whitecross and at the roundabout turn left on the A6124 into Musselburgh. The lodge is signposted on the left, and it should be noted that only the gardens are open.

Structure

The earliest portion of the house dates from 1683, and the whole was completed before 1700. The nucleus was an L-shaped structure, comprising a main block of two storeys and a garret in height, with a wing two storeys, an attic and a garret in height. Within the re-entrant angle, which opened to the north, was a semi-octagonal tower containing a turnpike. Shortly after its completion the wing was extended to the north-western boundary of the feu, and from this extension a low range of stabling was run up parallel to the main block. Within the re-entrant angle formed by the stair-tower and the extension an outbuilding was added in modern times.

The masonry was of rubble and is rough cast; the windows had dressed and back-set margins, which in the earlier work were moulded with an edge-roll and quirk, and in the later work chamfered at the arris; the window in the stair-tower above the entrance is dated 1683. The gables are crow-stepped.

The entrance is at the stairfoot in the north-eastern wall of the tower.

Brief History

The manors of Little Inveresk, having long been held by the monks of Dunfermline, were given by James VI, to the 1st Lord Maitland of Thirlestane, under whose grandson, the infamous Duke of Lauderdale, they suffered much curtailment.

Private residence. The gardens are in the care of The National Trust for Scotland and are open all year (admission charge) and from where the lodge can be seen.

Inveresk Lodge

26 Monkton House (*)

Ordnance Survey (OSR) = NT 334703

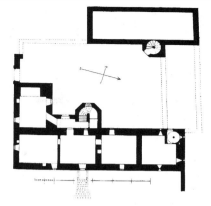

Continue on the A6124, and then turn left on the Inveresk Road and follow the road around to the traffic lights. Turn left at the lights and keep left with the river on the right. Drive over the river and turn left to Millerhill (or turn right to Newhailes — see page 199). Follow the B6415 towards Old Craighall. On exiting the village the house is on the left.

Monkton House – plan

Structure

The present structure is a commodious L-planned house, built about 1680 in extension of, and incorporating the lower part of, a 16th-century free-standing tower. As it stands the main house is a structure of three storeys, built of yellow freestone rubble, once harled but with dressed and back-set margins to the voids, the corners, and the eaves-courses. The basement floor only is vaulted.

The nucleus is thoroughly incorporated that it can only be traced from minor details

Brief History

A branch of the Hays of Yester succeeded the monks in the property, and it afterwards passed, on the forfeiture of the Hays in 1715, to the Falconers. At the end of the 19th century it belonged to Sir John Hope of Pinkie.

Private property but it can be viewed from the road.

Monkton House

27 Newton House (*)

Ordnance Survey (OSR) = NT 332699

> From Monkton continue on the B6415 for less than 200 yards then turn left into Newton Farm. The House is signed B & C Cowan.

Structure

The main house and doocot is 16th century, and has a barrel vault running the length of the ground floor, but has been considerably modernized. It appeared to have been oblong on plan with a projection on the northern side to contain a scale-and-platt staircase. The walling is of rubble and harled. The window margins were back-set and chamfered. On the east of the house and attached to it by a screen wall was a circular tower apparently of 16th century date. The lower storey was vaulted and had a gun loop opening southward. A narrow internal spiral staircase in the south-west corner was taken out, but you can still see the little blocked up windows.

Brief History

Sir William Murray of Newton, successor to another of the same name, appears in 1642 in a Presbytery case affecting a seat in the "Newton aisle" in the church, and again in 1664.

> It is a private residence, but the occupants of the buildings have no objection to anyone viewing the exterior of the house. However please respect their privacy and make a polite enquiry.

Newton House

28 Pinkie House (*)

Ordnance Survey (OSR) = NT 353727

Return to Musselburgh and go through the town centre. After the church Loretto School (Pinkie House) is on the right.

Structure

There was an L-planned house of the 16th century standing on the site, and this was incorporated and forms the northern end of the east wing. It comprised a vaulted substructure with two upper storeys.

The wing, which projected from the east range and belonged to the original house, was carried considerably above the main roof as a tower, and contained, besides a chamber on each floor, a spacious turnpike, which ascended to the second floor; the three tower rooms above were reached by a turret staircase, corbelled out in the north-west re-entrant angle, which rose to the platform roof, crested with an embattled parapet, where it terminated in a cap-house with an ogival roof.

It was built of rubble and once was harled.

Brief History

Originally it was erected by the abbots of Dunfermline as a hunting lodge towards the end of the 14th century, and occupied by them periodically up until the Reformation. The abbots were responsible for the massive central tower, built in the style popular at the time for defensive reasons and as a symbol of their power. The rooms to the north of the tower were added a hundred years later. It came into the hands of Alexander Seton, was the 3rd surviving son of George, 7th Lord Seton. He was raised from the bench to be Lord President of the Court of Session in 1593, was created Lord Fyvie in 1597, and Earl of Dunfermline in 1603. The King held him in high esteem, and when James VI went south to take up his crown, he committed into Seton's charge at Pinkie his eldest son Charles, who was later to become Charles I. In 1607 he married, as his third wife, Margaret Hay, daughter of James, 7th Lord Yester, and sister of John, 1st Earl of Tweeddale. He died at Pinkie in 1622. The 4th Earl of Dunfermline was forfeited in 1690 for adherence to James II, and it then passed to the first Marquess of

Pinkie House

Tweeddale, and by the 6th Marquess was sold in 1778 to Sir Archibald Hope of Craighall. His son, Sir John, succeeded to the title in 1801 at the age of 20, and it was he who was responsible for the first link between Pinkie and Loretto.

Permission should be sought from the school. Tel 0131 653 4444 or web www.lorettoschool.co.uk

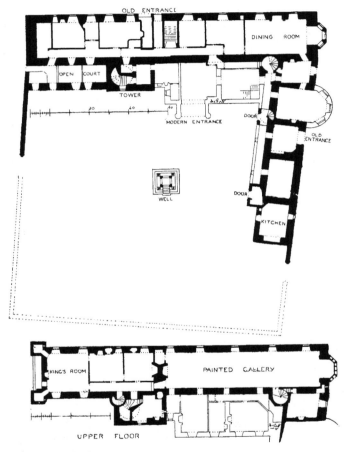

Pinkie House – plans

29 Fa'side Castle

Ordnance Survey (OSR) = NT 378710

Continue on the road to the roundabout and go straight across (North Berwick). Take the minor road to the right to Wallyford. Turn right at the junction and through Wallyford village. Pass over the A1 and take the first left. Driving up the hill take the first left which passes the castle. The road also takes you back to Tranent.

Structure

The 15th-century tower is the northern portion of the structure and is oblong on plan. The walls were of light coloured freestone rubble in parts roughly coursed. Oyster shell pinning was noted throughout. The voids, which had a broad chamfer on jambs and lintel, were filled in throughout the lower stages of the building. Several windows were altered in the 17th century. They had back-set margins slightly chamfered at jambs and lintel. The tower contained four storeys beneath the wall head, which was surmounted by a parapet walk; the uppermost storey only was vaulted, and this vault still appeared to be entire. The entrance was in the north wall at ground level through a doorway with a semicircular head, which admitted to a lobby, off which was entered the basement floor, and to a straight mural staircase ascending to the first floor; beneath the stair landing a prison or pit was contrived, the only access to which was a hatch.

Brief History

In the reign of David I (1124-53), William de Ffauside sat in the Scottish Parliament. The grant of Tranent Church by Thor to Holyrood circa 1150 was witnessed by, among others, Edmundo de Fazeside. In 1200 Allen de Fawside's name occurred in the Chartulary of Soltre, and 50 years later he gave an obligation to the monks of Dunfermline to pay out of his lands 5 solidi of silver. Robert de Fawside signed the Ragman Roll in 1292, and four years later Roger and William

Fa'side Castle

Fawsyde swore fealty to Edward I. "John of the hill of Fausyde" was a prisoner in Scarborough Castle in the early years of the 14th century.

In 1364 William de Fawsyde married Marjory, one of the daughters of Malcolm, Earl of Wigtown. September 1547 the castle witnessed its greatest historical event, the Battle of Pinkie, a day after there was a skirmish, the Battle of Little Fawside, where the English routed the Scottish cavalry. In 1582 Thomas Fawside sat on an assize, at which George Home of Spott was acquitted of the murder of Henry Stewart, Lord Darnley, husband of Mary, Queen of Scots.

Some time after 1631 Robert Fawside sold the estate to an Edinburgh merchant named Hamilton. The first Earl of Queensferry married Agnes, daughter of Fawsyde of Fawsyde in 1647, who was described as a member of an ancient family seated for four centuries at Fawside Castle.

It was probably uninhabited by 1798, and was bought as a ruin in 1976 by Mr and Mrs Tom Craig. They restored Fa'side Castle to the castle as seen today. Sadly Mr Craig died in January 2004.

It is a private property but it can be seen from the road. The present owners are members of the Scottish Castles Association and contribute to its visiting programme, which includes from time to time Fa'side Castle. They also commit themselves to the "Doors Open" day.

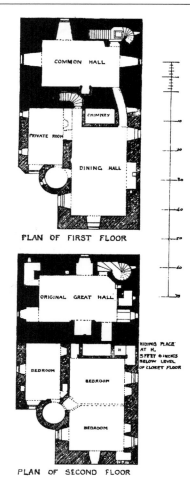

Fa'side Castle – plans

Castle Touring Guides

Midlothian

Map 4 – Midlothian

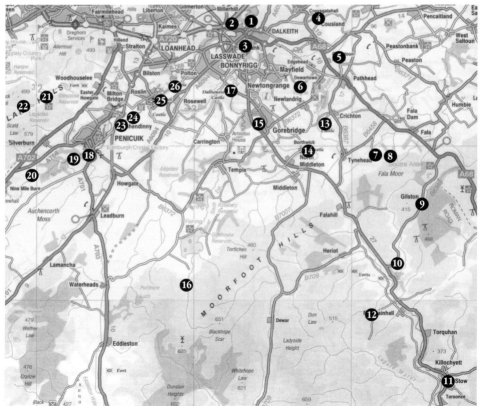

1 Dalkeith House

Ordnance Survey (OSR) = NT 333679

In the town, park at the east end of the High Street, outside Dalkeith Country Park (details of the Park on page 212). Turn left through the gates, and the older part of the building is at the rear.

Structure

The nucleus is a tower of about 15th century date, L-shaped on plan, which is incorporated in the present south wing. Part of the original ashlar masonry of this tower is seen from the roof of the modern kitchen extension, in the 10-foot wide stretch of red freestone, occurring at the level of the present first and upper floors. To the north of the tower lay a trapezoidal barmkin enclosed by curtains furnished with crenellated parapets. This was entered, probably over a ditch, through a gatehouse placed towards the middle of the north wall. The curtain had a heavy projecting base-course, and a small portion of this remains within the basement, on the north. In the 16th century and later the curtains were partly rebuilt.

Brief History

The Anglo-Norman knight, William de Graham, a witness to the foundation charter of Holyrood Abbey (1128), received from David I the manor of Dalkeith; his seventh descendant, John de Graham, dying without issue about the middle of the 14th century, left two sisters, his heiresses, of whom one, Marjory, conveyed Dalkeith by marriage to the Douglases. In 1452 the town was plundered and burned by the brother of the murdered 6th Earl of Douglas, but the castle held out under Patrick Cockburn, its governor; in 1458 James II, conferred on James Douglas of Dalkeith the title of Earl of Morton; and at the 2nd Earl's castle James IV first met his affianced Queen, Princess Margaret of England. In 1543 Cardinal Beaton was committed prisoner here; and in 1547 it had to yield to the English victors at Pinkie. James, 4th Earl of Morton, the cruel and grasping Regent, built at Dalkeith about 1575 a magnificent palace.

Francis Scott, 2nd Earl of Buccleuch, purchased Dalkeith from the 9th Earl of Morton in 1642. Dying in 1651, he left two daughters, Mary and Anne, who, successively Countesses of Buccleuch in their own right, married, at the early ages of 11 and 12, Walter Scott of Highchester and the ill-fated Duke of Monmouth, both of them only 14.

The exterior is freely accessible within the Park, which is open April-September daily. The house is not open.

Dalkeith House

2 Sheriffhall (*)

Ordnance Survey (OSR) = NT 320680

Return from the Country Park along the High Street to the traffic lights. Turn right on the A68 (Edinburgh). Just before the next set of traffic lights, turn right on to the entrance area in front of the gateway, and park. Sheriffhall can be seen looking north.

Structure

The late 16th- or early 17th-century house of Sheriffhall was demolished, with the exception of the stair-wing. It is a square rubble-built structure. The original entrance had a moulded door piece, and above it an empty panel-space. At first floor level there are gun-loops to the south and east.

Brief History

The lands of Sheriffhall had belonged to the Abbey of Dunfermline and were occupied by a family named Gifford before and after the Reformation.

The tower is readily seen from the highway.

Sheriffhall

3 Newbattle Abbey

Ordnance Survey (OSR) = NT 333660

the Earl of Hertford. The last abbot, Mark Ker, was made the first commendator of Newbattle in 1564.

Retrace your steps to Dalkeith, and turn right at the High Street traffic lights. Continue to the first roundabout, and take the first left on the B703. At the next mini-roundabout go straight on, and the College is a further 500 yards on the left.

The Abbey College can be seen from the highway. If you require to enter the grounds please contact the Principal at the College. Tel 0131 663 1921 or web www.newbattleabbeycollege.ac.uk

Structure

Only small portions of the old buildings now remain, and of those the most important is the fratery, with its central row of columns and vaulted roof.

Brief History

David I founded the monastery in 1140 for a colony of Cistercian monks from Melrose. Alexander II obtained a grave there for his consort, Mary. In 1385 the abbey was burned during the inroad of Richard II; and in 1544, during James Hasmall's abbacy, was burned again by

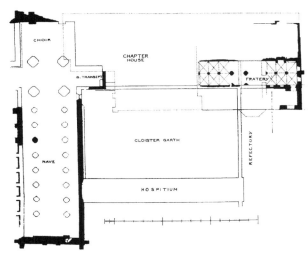

Newbattle Abbey – plan

Newbattle Abbey

4 Cousland Tower (*)

Ordnance Survey (OSR) = NT 377683

Return to Dalkeith, and turn right at the first set of traffic lights (before entering the centre of town). Bear right on the A68 at the mini-roundabout; straight on at the next mini-roundabout, and up the hill. Drive passed Fordell Services and turn left signposted Cousland. Go straight across at the T-junction, and on entering the village the original walling is on the left. Turn right at the T-junction, and after 125 yards the ruins are on the right.

Structure

The remains now form an enclosure, which was undoubtedly a garden or orchard, and the masonry suggests 17th-century work. At the north-east corner was a very ruinous late 16th-century house, of which the part that projected within the enclosure appeared to be earlier than the portion lying parallel to and incorporated in the east wall. Its basement was ceiled with a barrel-vault, beneath which, at springing level, was a timber floor with joists borne on massive corbels that project from the wall face. The entrance was in the south wall immediately south of the enclosure, and of it one jamb remained.

Brief History

The Duke of Somerset, in 1547, on his way to Fawside Hill and the subsequent Battle of Pinkie, took possession of Cousland and its castle en route. Twenty years later, Bothwell and some 2000 men marched to Carberry Hill; and the next day took up the position on the ill-fated field of Pinkie, later they swept round by Smeaton to camp beneath the walls of the ruined Cousland Castle. Bothwell rode off to Dunbar leaving Mary to surrender there.

Cousland belonged to the St. Clairs of Roslin. In 1656 Robert MacGill, son of Sir James MacGill of Cranston-Riddell, was returned heir to his brother in the lands and barony of Cousland.

The ruins can be seen from the roadside.

Cousland Tower

5 Oxenfoord Castle (*)

Ordnance Survey (OSR) = NT 388656

Return and turn left up Southfield Road. Turn left at the junction on the A6124, and then left again on the A68. The entrance to the castle is signed on the left after 1.5 miles.

Structure

This seat of the Earl of Stair dates from 1780, having been remodelled by Robert Adam, but was considerably enlarged at a later time by William Burn. Encased within it is the shell of a 16th-century tower, hardly to be traced in the building, but clearly shown on Adam's plans. The tower was L-shaped on plan, and within the re-entrant angle was a stair-tower. There was no parapet. At the angles were turrets containing little "studies". There were four storeys, the basement of both main block and wing being vaulted.

Brief History

The estate, called formerly Oxford, from 1661 till 1706, gave the title of Viscount Oxfurd, in the peerage of Scotland, to the family of Macgill, whose heiress, Elizabeth, in 1760 married her cousin, Sir John Dalrymple of Cousland, a great-great-grandson of the first Viscount Stair. Their son, Sir John, in 1853 succeeded as 8th Earl of Stair.

To view the castle permission must be sought from the owner. Grounds open occasionally to the public as part of Scotland's Gardens Scheme. (www.gardensofscotland.org)

Oxenfoord Castle

6 Southsyde Castle (*)

Ordnance Survey (OSR) = NT 369638

On exiting Oxenfoord, go straight across on the B6372 (Gorebridge). Turn right signed Edgehead, and then take the first left, and Southsyde is nearly 0.5 miles on the left hand side.

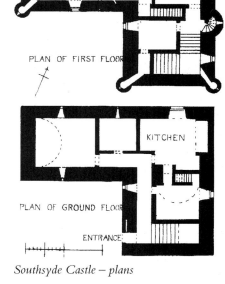

PLAN OF FIRST FLOOR

KITCHEN

PLAN OF GROUND FLOOR

ENTRANCE

Southsyde Castle – plans

Structure

It is a 17th-century rubble built structure. On plan it is L-shaped and originally four storeys in height, but now reduced to three. The original entrance was at the southern end of the west wall.

Brief History

The various lands of Southsyde were united into a barony and de novo granted by the king in 1644 to Patrick Eleis of Plewlands, thereafter known as Southsyde.

The property can be seen from the road.

Southsyde Castle

7 Cakemuir Castle (*)

Ordnance Survey (OSR) = NT 413591

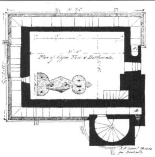

Cakemuir Castle – plan

Return to the T-junction in Edgehead, turn right and straight across the junction into Ford. Turn right in Pathhead on the A68. After 2.5 miles, turn right on the B6458. After 500 yards take the left fork on an unclassified road. Continue south for 500 yards to the end of the road where Cakemuir can be seen.

Structure

This structure is a mid 16th-century tower, and oblong on plan. It has a turret, circled on plan for the greater part of its height, projecting from the north wall to contain the stair. From the west wall there projected an 18th-century wing, which in its turn was added to in recent years. Below the wall-head the tower contained four storeys, which were reached by a spacious wheel-stair. A parapet surmounted the wall-head with walk borne on moulded corbels, which butted against the stair-tower, which developed to an oblong on plan and terminated in a cap-house with crow-stepped gables. In the west gable, on either side of the chimney, was a roofed watch-box with a stone seat for the occupant. The only provision for defence was a series of gun-loops on the fourth floor.

On the outside of the east gable was placed a panel, which was removed from above the original entrance. It had a shield bearing the Wauchope arms – a chevron between two mullets in chief and a garb in base.

Brief History

It has a Queen Mary's room, having given shelter to that unfortunate queen after her flight in male apparel from Borthwick on 13th June 1567. Here she met Bothwell, and rode with him through the night to Dunbar.

Cakemuir Castle

8 Fala Luggie Tower (*)

Ordnance Survey (OSR) = NT 425590

Retrace your steps to the A68 and turn right. Drive for 1.25 miles, and just after the B6457 right turn is a turn left on a track. Drive to the gate and park. The ruined tower is about 1 mile along the track.

Structure

It is a fragment of a structure dating from the late 16th or early 17th century, which was oblong on plan. The masonry is of rubble with freestone dressings. The south-east wall is the only portion standing. Evidence suggests that it was at least three storeys in height. The basement was ceiled with appointed barrel vault. The first floor had two small windows with a southern aspect.

The ruin is freely accessible.

Fala Luggie Tower

9 Gilston Peel

Ordnance Survey (OSR) = NT 443562

Rejoin the A68 from Fala Luggie, and turn right. After 1.5 miles, turn right on the B6368 and after 2 miles it can be seen on the right. Please note that Soutra Aisle is on the left 1.25 miles before Gilston.

Structure

Little remains of the 16th-century tower house, which has been incorporated into a later building. At the time of going to press it is clearly undergoing renovation with a view to occupation.

The renovation is by the roadside.

Gilston Peel

10 Crookston Old House

Ordnance Survey (OSR) = NT 425522

Continue on B6368 (the site of Kaythe Castle is just after Nether Brotherstone Farm, 1.25 miles from Gilston, on the south side of the bridge). Crookston is a further 1.25 miles on the left.

Structure

Built by the Borthwicks around 1446, it incorporates a 15th-century keep. It was extended in the 17th century, again in the 19th century, and is now a T-plan house of three storeys and a garret.

Can be seen from the road.

Crookston Old House

11 Bishop's Palace, Stow (*)

Ordnance Survey (OSR) = NT 460445

> Continue on the B6368 to the A7. Turn left and drive for 5 miles to the village of Stow. Take the next left after B6362 up a narrow lane and the ruined palace is on the left.

Structure

It is an oblong structure lying with its major axis north-west and south-east. The walls are built of grey-wacke rubble in narrow courses. The gables are fairly complete, but the lateral walls have mainly been destroyed. It originally had three storeys and a garret and of the late 15th and early 16th century.

Brief History

It was the property of the bishops and later archbishops of St Andrews.

> The ruin is freely accessible in the village of Stow.

Bishop's Palace, Stow

12 Howliston Tower

Ordnance Survey (OSR) = NT 412489

Return to the A7 and turn right. Take the first left opposite the B6362, cross the Gala Water and turn right at the T-junction. Head north for nearly 4 miles and then turn left at the junction to Pirntaton. In 1 mile the ruin is in a farmstead.

Structure

Little remains of a tower house built into the farm.

Brief History

It was the property of the Home family in 1626, but had passed to the Mitchells by 1690.

The ruin can be seen from the track.

Howliston Tower

13 Crichton Castle (*)

Ordnance Survey (OSR) = NT 380612

Return to the junction, and turn left. Drive for 3 miles and then join the B709 just before Heriot village. Turn right through Heriot, travel for about 1.25 miles and turn left on the A7. After 2 miles take the right turn on the B6367 signed Crichton. It is 3 miles to the village of Crichton. Here, turn left at the T-junction, and then take the left fork. Park at the church and walk to the castle.

Structure

The buildings completely enclose a courtyard, and are set at the north-west angle of the site. The various portions have been built at different periods, but the nucleus is a late 14th-century tower in the centre of the eastern side, which is the original house and a self-contained unit. Two wings were added in the 15th century and formed the south and west sides of a courtyard, of which the northern side may have been a screen wall or another wing afterwards removed or reconstructed. The present northern range dates from the period 1581-91.

Within it are a basement and a mezzanine floor beneath a semi-circular barrel-vault, and on the first floor a hall below a lofty pointed barrel-vault. Above this there has been at least one other storey. There is no internal communication save between the first and upper floors.

Brief History

A Turstan de Creichton was one of the witnesses to the charter of foundation of Holyrood Abbey (1128); his most famous descendant was Sir William Crichton, the founder of both castle and church, who, as chancellor of Scotland, was alternately rival and friend of Sir Alexander Livingston, and who in 1440 at Edinburgh Castle beheaded the young Earl of Douglas and his brother – an act of treachery for which his own fortress was taken and dismantled by the Douglases. In 1445 Sir William was made Lord Crichton, the third holder of which title lost its estates in 1484 for joining Albany against James III.

Crichton Castle

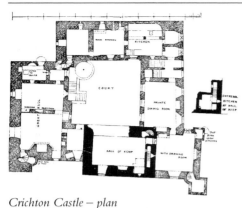

Crichton Castle – plan

Hepburn, 1st Earl of Bothwell, by whose great-grandson, Darnley's murderer, they were once more forfeited in 1567. Nine years later James VI bestowed them on his ill-starred cousin, Francis Stewart, 5th Earl of Bothwell; and subsequently they passed through the hands of a dozen proprietors, from one of whom, Hepburn of Humbie (1649), the castle was nicknamed Humbie's Wa's, till at last they came to the Callendars. Queen Mary feasted in the castle hall, on occasion of the marriage here of her natural brother, Sir John Stewart.

After four years' tenure by the minion Ramsay, they were granted in 1488 to Patrick

It is the care of Historic Scotland, and open during the summer. Admission charge. Tel 01875 320017.

Crichton Castle

14 Borthwick Castle (*)

Ordnance Survey (OSR) = NT 370597

Return to the village of Crichton, take the first sharp left, and drive through the wooded area. There is a superb view of Crichton Castle and the church to the left. At the crossroads turn left. After 400 yards take the right fork. Borthwick is seen left across the valley. After 400 yards turn left signed Borthwick, and park outside the church.

Structure

The finest of Scottish castles built on the model of the keep. The general plan of the main block is a parallelogram, containing the great hall; but in this case, instead of one projecting wing, there are two wings. The outer walls enclose a courtyard of irregular form. These walls stand at the top of steep banks, at the bottom of which there is a ditch. The angles and curtains are defended with towers and bastions. The gatehouse has had a drawbridge and outer gate, as well as a portcullis in the inner archway.

Brief History

In June 1430 Sir William de Borthwick received a special license to construct and fortify a castle or fortalice in the place commonly called the Mote of Lochorwart. Thomas Hay of Lochorwart and this William Borthwick had been members of this assize at the trial in 1423 when the Duke of Albany and his son were condemned to death. Borthwick was a substitute hostage in England from July 1425 under the treaty for the liberation of James I, and was kept in York Castle, being released during 1427. On 10th June 1567 the insurgent lords suddenly appeared before Borthwick Castle, where Queen Mary was with her husband, but Bothwell had been warned and had ridden off the night before, leaving Mary with six or

Borthwick Castle

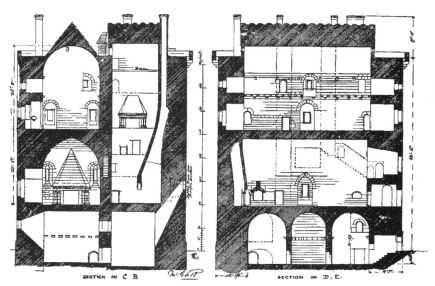

Borthwick Castle – sections

seven of her attendants, whereupon the lords withdrew to Edinburgh.

The 10th Lord Borthwick held the castle against Cromwell in 1650.

Borthwick Castle is a hotel, and is open to non-residents. Tel 01875 820514 or web www.borthwickcastlehotel.co.uk

15 Newbyres Tower (*)

Ordnance Survey (OSR) = NT 344614

Continue on the minor road until it meets the A7. Turn right and after 0.75 miles turn right again on the B6372/B704 (Station Road). Turn left into the Health Centre car park – the lower level, and follow the path in an unkempt area facing the housing estate, not the tarmacked footpath. The ruin is about 25 yards away in the overgrown patch.

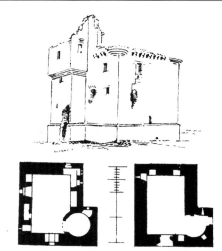

Newbyres Tower – c. 1890 and plans

Structure

The site of this mid 16th-century tower is roughly triangular and lies with its apex south-south-east; its flanks were defined and naturally defended by deeply worn water-courses, and along the base there appeared to have been a courtyard wall. In the middle of this area the ruin stands. On plan it has been an L-shaped building. The wing, which housed the staircase, lay at the southern angle. The masonry is of rubble, with freestone dressings set in hard mortar with shell pinnings. The tower contained three storeys beneath the wall-head and an attic storey within the parapet.

The other defensive features were the four gun-loops. The entrance, which was usually placed within the re-entrant angle, appeared to have been in the south wall of the wing.

Brief History

In 1621 James Borthwick of Newbyres was returned heir to his father, John Borthwick of Newbyres.

It is freely accessible.

Newbyres Tower

16 Hirendean Castle (*)

Ordnance Survey (OSR) = NT 298512

Go out of the car park, turn right and return to the A7. Cross over on the B6372 and continue south-west for approximately 5 miles. At a sharp right hand turn, turn left signed Gladhouse Reservoir. Drive south for 1 mile and then turn left signed Moorfoot, and then park on the left side overlooking the reservoir. Continue on foot to Moorfoot Farm, and turn right. The ruin is 500 yards on the left.

Structure

The structure was built of irregularly coursed rubble and is oblong on plan. Only the south wall and a fragment of the west gable remained; these showed that the building had at least three storeys; the lowest of which was ceiled with a stone barrel-vault. The masonry was inferior, and the long and short quoins were undressed; the freestone jambs of the windows and of the entrance at the west end of the south wall, though dressed, were unmoulded.

Brief History

The lands of "Herringden" belonged to the Abbey of Newbattle. A charter of confirmation to Robert, Earl of Lothian, in 1620, included Hirendean. In 1649 Patrick Scot was returned heir to his father, William Scot.

It is freely accessible.

Hirendean Castle

17 Dalhousie Castle (*)

Ordnance Survey (OSR) = NT 320636

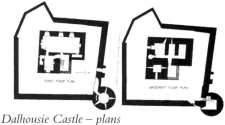

Dalhousie Castle – plans

(This is the nearest major castle to Arniston House – see page 198). From Hirendean, return to the A7, and turn left. After 1.25 miles turn left at the traffic lights into the B704 (Bonnyrigg). Dalhousie Castle Hotel is over the bridge and turn right.

Structure

The castle incorporates an altered 16th-century L-plan tower house, within a 13th-century courtyard with corner towers and a moat, traces of which remain. The main entrance, through a tall archway, is crowned by two bartizans, and a large round tower survives, at one corner, from the courtyard. In the 17th century the castle was extended, and William Burn made further substantial internal alterations in 1820. The slots for the drawbridge survive.

Brief History

In the first half of the 12th century Simon de Ramsay received a grant of lands in Midlothian from David I; in 1296 and 1304 William de Ramsay swore fealty to Edward I for the lands of Dalwolzie. His son, Sir Alexander, was one of the great Scottish leaders in the Wars of Independence, the capturer of Roxburgh, who for reward was starved to death in the Castle of Hermitage (1342); in 1400 his namesake and fourth descendant successfully defended Dalhousie against Henry IV of England. This Sir Alexander was slain at Homildon (1402), as was another at Flodden (1513). In 1618 George Ramsay, eleventh in descent from the first Sir Alexander, was raised to the peerage as Lord Ramsay of Melrose; and in 1633 his son and successor, William, was created Earl of Dalhousie and Baron Ramsay of Kerington. Oliver Cromwell addressed his letters from Dalhousie.

Hotel so permission should be sought to view. Tel 01875 820153 or web www.dalhousiecastle.co.uk

Dalhousie Castle

18 Uttershill Castle (*)

Ordnance Survey (OSR) = NT 235594

Return to the B704 and turn right. At the traffic lights turn left on the A6094. After 4.5 miles turn right on the B6372 and in about 600 yards turn right on the B7026 and then immediate left on the B6372 again. Uttershill is a further 600 yards on the left. It can be recommended that before you take the right hand turn from the A6094, continue into the village of Howgate. Turn left at the junction and the Howgate Inn is 500 yards on the left, and serves superb meals, wines etc at a value for money price.

Structure

It is the ruin of a late 16th-century mansion. It was oblong on plan, and was at least three storeys in height. The walls were of freestone rubble, once probably harled. An entrance in the south wall at ground level had a moulded and rather well proportioned architrave and cornice. The north and west windows had rounded arrises at jambs and lintels, while the south and east windows had a bold quirked edge-roll.

The entrance opened on a small lobby, which contained the remains of a scale-stair ascending to the first floor. From this lobby was entered on the west a vaulted cellar, which was the only vaulted portion of the structure.

Brief History

It was the manor of the barony of Preston or Gorton, and so belonged to the Prestons of Craigmillar. The father of Sir John Clerk of Penicuik bought Uttershill in 1702.

There is some consolidation work being carried out, but it is freely visible with care.

Uttershill Castle

19 Ravensneuk Castle (*)

Ordnance Survey (OSR) = NT 224590

Continue down the hill to the T-junction, and turn left on the A701 (Peebles). Turn right into Alderbank and park there. Follow the track for 750 yards.

Structure

Its remains consisted only of the north wall with a portion of the gable returns. These were built of freestone rubble and are less than six feet high. The western half of the north wall was unvaulted. The eastern portion appears to be older and is vaulted. It contained an inlet for water with an external dished stone basin, indicating that the kitchen was at this end of the building on the ground floor.

Brief History

The lands of Ravensneuk belonged to the Sinclairs of Roslin. One owner, Oliver Sinclair, was commander-in-chief of the forces in the time of James V. In 1730 Sir John Clerk of Penicuik bought Easter and Wester Ravensnook.

The ruin is freely accessible.

Ravensneuk Castle

20 Brunstane Castle (*)

Ordnance Survey (OSR) = NT 201582

> Exit the car park from Ravensneuk, and turn left on the A701 to Penicuik. Turn left on the A766 (Carlisle), and after 2.5 miles turn left to Brunstane Farm. The castle can be seen through the farm area.

Brunstane Castle

Structure

This ruin of a fair-sized mansion, built on a courtyard plan by Alexander Crichton in 1542-4, and rebuilt by his son in 1568. The remains are extensive. The area enclosed and built on is roughly oblong in shape. The southern and western sides were formed by ranges of building, which abutted at the north-eastern angle on a free-standing rectangular tower. The north wall has not survived, but in it there must have been the gateway, which gave entrance to the courtyard. The masonry of the structure was rubble-built. The ample provision of gun-loops is noteworthy; these were oval in form.

Brief History

In 1373, David of Penycuke, for good service and advice rendered to him, granted to his cousin, William of Crichtoune, the whole lands of Brunston and Welchton. These lands were to be held by the said William and Thomas of Crichtoune, his son, and failing the latter by death without leaving lawful heirs of his body, by Edward Crichtoune, his brother.

> The castle ruins are in the middle of a working farm, therefore access is only on foot and entirely at the visitor's own risk.

Brunstane Castle

21 Logan House (*)

Ordnance Survey (OSR) = NT 204630

On exiting Brunstane, turn left on the A766, and then turn right on the A702 (Edinburgh). After 5 miles turn left just beyond Flotterstone Inn, and then turn right in front of the inn, and then right again into the car park of the Pentland Hills Regional Park. Walk up Glen Road for 2.5 miles to the remnants of Logan House on the right.

Structure

The 16th-century ruins stand besides a cottage on the left bank of the Logan Burn. The structure had been a square tower, whose walls were of rubble with freestone dressings, enclosing the ground floor, a single apartment ceiled with a barrel-vault. The entrance was in the centre of the north wall and was flanked internally by a small cupboard on either side.

There appears to have been only one small window on this floor, set in the south wall immediately opposite the doorway. There is no trace of a staircase. The north-east angle of the tower was set back to receive a gate, which was, apparently, the entrance to the courtyard north of the building.

Brief History

In 1410 Henry, Earl of Orkney and Lord of St. Clair, granted to his brother the lands of Logan House with pertinents in Pentland Moor. In 1542 the king confirmed to Sir William Sinclair of Roslin a grant, including "Loganehous" with the tower. In 1593 the laird of Roslin informed the Synod of Edinburgh "his residence was in the Loganhouse tower". One of its owners was Charles Cowan, Liberal M.P for Edinburgh (1847-59).

The scant ruins are visible from the side of the path.

Logan House

22 Howlet's House (*)

Ordnance Survey (OSR) = NT 194625

Continue on from Logan House and the ruins of Howlet's House are a further 600 yards onwards.

Structure

At the southern base lies this ruinous structure, dating probably from the end of the 16th century, standing on a triangular and fairly level promontory. The walls, which are of rubble and still stand up to 15-feet high, show that the lowest storey was ceiled with a barrel-vault. In the side walls were small windows.

The ruin is freely accessible.

Howlet's House

23 Auchindinny House

Ordnance Survey (OSR) = NT 252613

From Howlet's House, return back to the main road, and turn right on the A702. In 500 yards turn left signed Mauricewood, and then take the first left fork. At the A701 junction go straight across signed Auchendinny. At the next junction with the B7026 turn right and drive through the village. On exiting the village Auchindinny House is the last entrance on the left.

Structure
The small mansion with flanking pavilions, designed by Sir William Bruce, and dating from about 1705, incorporates two vaulted chambers from an earlier house.

Brief History
It was a property of the Inglis family from 1702, and they built the present house.

Can be seen from the highway.

Auchindinny House

24 Old Woodhouselee (*)

Ordnance Survey (OSR) = NT 258617

Return through Auchendinny village to where you joined it from Howlet's House. On the right there is a works road (Dalmore Mill). Park and follow the public footpath through the Mill grounds for 400 yards. The ruin is on a promontory above the river on the right hand side.

Woodhouselee, should be repossessed in the lands. In 1601 Sir James Ballantyne of Broughton made complaint that David Hamilton, younger of Bothwellhaugh, and his accomplices had threatened his tenants at Woodhouselee. In 1607 William Ballantyne served heir to his father, Sir James Ballantyne of Broughton.

Freely accessible.

Structure

On the ground floor there is a ruinous oblong range containing three vaulted and intercommunicating cellars lit by small windows in the haunches of the vaults. At the first floor level a small wing projected and was founded on the higher ground above the cleft, so that the structure at this and higher levels was L-shaped on plan. The walls of the wing are reduced to the foundations.

Brief History

Woodhouselee is said to have been the property of the wife of James Hamilton of Bothwellhaugh, the assassin of the Regent Moray in 1570. Her eviction in most cruel circumstances is given as one motive for his action, the estate having been granted to Sir John Ballenden or Ballantyne, twice Justice Clerk. On 12th January 1591 the Privy Council declared that David Hamilton of Bothwellhaugh, Isobel Sinclair and Alison Sinclair, heirs-portioners of the lands of

Old Woodhouselee

25 Rosslyn Castle (*)

Ordnance Survey (OSR) = NT 274628

during Hertford's invasion, and after being partially restored after 1580, was again injured in 1650 by General Monk. In the 16th and early 17th centuries it was a favourite haunt of gypsies.

Return to the B7026 and turn right and drive through Auchendinny. Before the A701 (Roslin Glen Hotel) turn right, signed Roslin. At T-junction turn right, and then turn right on the bend to Rosslyn Chapel. Turn right into the car park. Before leaving spend some time in Rosslyn Chapel.

The habitable part of the main building is let out via the Landmark Trust, but the exterior is freely accessible. Landmark Trust telephone 01628 825925 or web www.landmarktrust.org.uk

Structure

The oldest part of the present building is a peel tower to the south east of the entrance and erected by Sir William St Clair. Henry, the 2nd Earl of Orkney, added the donjon tower about 60 years later. Above the gateway was a gatehouse with round turrets facing the bridge, of which the corbelling and some courses of masonry still remain.

Brief History

Sir William St Clair was one of the band of knights who set out with Bruce's heart to Palestine, and who fell fighting against the Moors in 1330. The greater part of the castle was destroyed by fire in 1452, but it must have been repaired very quickly, as it was chosen as the prison of Sir William Hamilton, who had been involved in the Douglas rebellion. In 1544 it was almost totally destroyed by the English,

Rosslyn Castle

26 Hawthornden Castle (*)

Ordnance Survey (OSR) = NT 287637

From Rosslyn Chapel use the footpath to walk down to the river. Going north-westwards Hawthornden is about 1 mile along the river side on the right. Return to the main road, and turn right on the A701 and then the A768 to return to Dalkeith.

Structure

The oldest part was a 15th-century tower, quadrangular in plan and containing at least three storeys. It is now entered form the courtyard, and opened into the basement which had a single chamber ceiled with a barrel vault. The west wall does not exist above the vault.

Brief History

William Drummond, the Scottish Petrarch, was born here on 13th December 1585. He entertained Ben Jonson at Hawthornden in 1618-9, after Jonson had walked from London to Edinburgh; and here, broken hearted by Charles I's execution, Drummond died on 4th December 1649. Sir James Hamlyn Williams-Drummond bought the property in 1828. There are some curious artificial caves in the grounds with names such as King's Gallery, King's Bedchamber and King's Dining-room; and they were occupied in 1338 as military retreats by the band of Sir Alexander Ramsay of Dalhousie. Queen Victoria also visited them.

The castle is run as an International Retreat for Writers and, as such, permission to view is unlikely to be granted.

© Crown Copyright: RCAHMS

Hawthornden Castle

Castle Touring Guides

West Lothian

Map 5 – West Lothian

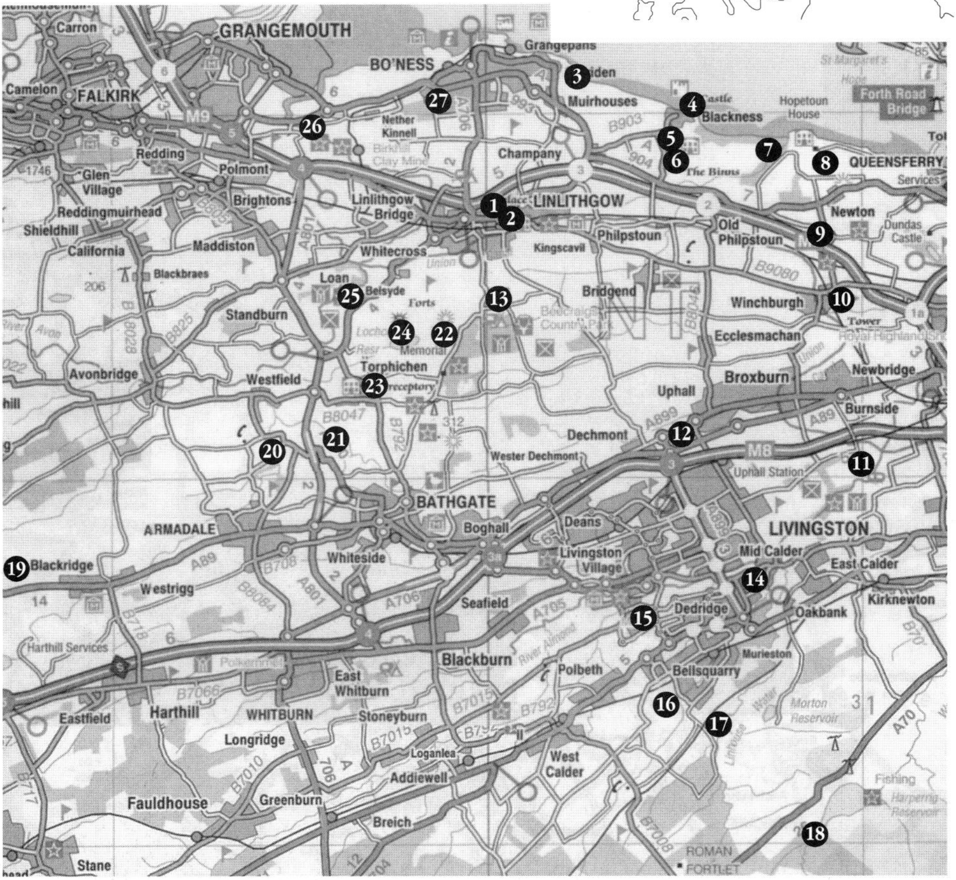

Scotland

Dundee

Glasgow Edinburgh

© Philip's 2003, © Crown copyright 2003

1 Linlithgow Palace (*)

Ordnance Survey (OSR) = NT 003774

> In the centre of Linlithgow, follow the signs to the Palace, and park there.

Structure

On this site there stood in the 12th century a manor house of the king and this structure was incorporated in 1301-2 into the peel built by Edward I. In the reign of David II the manor house was built anew, and it was again rebuilt at the end of the 14th century, only to be destroyed by fire in 1424. From the reconstruction have grown the present buildings.

The masonry is of two main types; one dating from the 15th century comprises the lower part of the outer walls, fairly cubical and regularly coursed; the other, 16th and 17th century work, is close set ashlar, regularly coursed. The lowest part of the present east wall and the footing returning westward from the north-east angle to the north of the

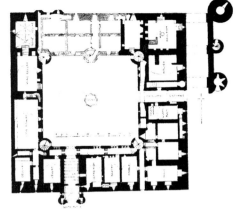

Linlithgow Palace – plan

present building line may be the remains of the house burnt down in 1424. As a result of a major reconstruction initiated by James IV and completed by James V prior to his first marriage, the palace became established as a symmetrical structure both in plan and in elevation.

The main entrance, inserted before 1534, in still earlier walling, lies between two fine late Gothic niches and is slightly set back, beneath a cuspated head to receive the

Linlithgow Palace

drawbridge when raised.

Brief History

The first of the Scottish kings who made it a favourite residence was Robert II. In 1388 he held a parliament here, and in 1389 he granted to the burgh the earliest charter now remaining in its archives. From the reign of Robert II down to that of James VI, the castle and palace were very frequently visited by the court. Under the Regent Albany and James I, the town was twice burned, first in 1411 and again in 1424, in the latter the castle was also injured, and in 1425 the earlier portions of the present palace were begun. James III married in 1468 to Margaret of Denmark, and James IV married Margaret of England here. In 1517 Stirling and his followers who had attempted to assassinate Meldrum of Binns fled to Linlithgow.

It is in the care of Historic Scotland and is open all year round. Admission charge. Tel 01506 842896.

Linlithgow Palace

2 West Port (*)

Ordnance Survey (OSR) = NT 002770

On exiting the Palace car park, turn right through town. West Port is on the left hand side, just before the right turn (B706 – Bo'ness).

Structure

It is a large L-shaped tenement of three storeys, completed in 1600, James Hamilton being the owner, and was originally part of the wall which surrounded Linlithgow town and the Palace. It is believed that Mary of Guise lived here and planted an oak tree in the garden. It became a "monster" and had to be cut down as it totally overshadowed the house.

Brief History

It was the property of the Hamiltons. Hamilton of Bothwellhaugh shot and killed the Regent Moray in 1570 from a house nearby, after Moray had turned his wife and baby out from their home at Old Woodhouselee.

The building is easily viewed from the road.

West Port House

3 Carriden House

Ordnance Survey (OSR) = NT 026808

Continue on the B706. (After 500 yards where the road widens there is a footpath to the right where there good views of the Palace across the loch.) Drive for 2.5 miles, then turn right at the traffic lights (Dean Road) on the A993. A further 1.5 miles before turning left on Carriden Brae. Take the third right turn and the House is at the end of the lane.

Structure

The eastern part, though considerably altered, dates at least from the 17th century and could be as early as the 16th century. It was L-shaped on plan, lying with the re-entrant facing south-west. In height there are four storeys above a vaulted basement. At each of the five outer angles were turrets carried on the usual conoidal corbelling; these were provided with fluted gun-holes. The upper windows had been provided with oblong gun-loops in their sills. Where unaltered, the windows are rounded or moulded with a quirked edge-roll at jamb and lintel. The masonry was coursed rubble.

History

The oldest part is the eastern tower, built by John Hamilton of Letterick (later the 1st Lord Bargany) in 1602, although he is thought to have incorporated parts of an earlier building.

Patrick Abercromby's son (also Patrick) sold Carriden to John Hamilton of Letterick in 1601 and the next year John built the existing stone tower house. The 1602 tower was L-shaped, mainly rubble-built and on five floors, the lowest level being vaulted. John's son, the 2nd Lord Bargany, sold the house in 1667, and it passed through a number of hands. From 1678 it belonged to several generations of the Mylne family. The mid-18th century saw enthusiasm for grandiose landscaping schemes, and in around 1750 up to a metre of soil was added to the gardens surrounding the house to level the ground. In 1766 the then owner persuaded Carriden Kirk Session to rebuild the church on a site beside the shore to the northwest.

Carriden House

Carriden House

Admiral Sir George Johnstone Hope bought Carriden in 1814. Admiral Hope had fought with Nelson at the Battle of Trafalgar, commanding the 74-gun battleship *Defence*. He died in 1829, and was succeeded by his son James, who also rose to become Admiral of the Fleet, seeing action in South America and China. During the 1840s, after some years working at the Admiralty in London, he chose to retire to his father's estate at Carriden. But first he took the opportunity to remodel Carriden House to his taste. It was extensively rebuilt inside and out in a Scottish Baronial style, rather like that of the renowned architect William Burn, rich in turrets, battlements, bay and oriel windows and a slate roof (earlier stone roof tiles are occasionally dug up in the garden). The original architect is unknown, and it is unclear as to whether any of the numerous gun loops date from before 1846. The rebuilding extended to other parts of the estate, with various estate offices, workers' cottages, stables and a coach house, and a new village (now the Muirhouses conservation village). The only one of Hope's new buildings on land still attached to the house is a rather impressive underground icehouse in the wooded north-facing slope behind the house.

Carriden passed after James' death through various scions of the Hope family including, between 1890 and the First World War, to the Lloyd Verney's.

The house also operates as a "Bed & Breakfast" using 5 large en-suite rooms. Weddings are occasionally accommodated (the local minister is happy to oblige) - though for anything more than about 25 guests it is recommended using a marquee on the lawn in addition to the house. Contact the house on 01506 829811 or browse the website www.carridenhouse.co.uk (under construction at time of writing) for further details. The owners are members of the Scottish Castles Association, and the Events Programme may include Carriden House from time to time.

4 Blackness Castle (*)

Ordnance Survey (OSR) = NT 056803

> Return to the A993 and turn left after 1 mile on the B903. The village is 2 miles further on where you can park or at the castle car park.

Structure

Named after the low narrow promontory, the Black Ness, it closely resembles the deck of a ship. Within the enclosure is the mid-tower, a freestanding tower house built of rubble of the 15th century. It was originally square on plan, but in 1667, when it was to be used as a prison, a turnpike-tower was thrown out from the north-east angle. The original staircase was probably at the same angle and entirely contained within the thickness of the wall. In 1693 the wall-heads with their parapet and walk were removed, but corbels for angle-rounds still remain at three corners. There were five storeys, all considerably altered for use as stores. The basement had been vaulted, but the vault no longer exists, while only one original window remained, that to the north, which had a stepped breast.

Brief History

It was burned in 1443-4, amid the conflicts of the Douglases, Livingstons, Crichtons and Forresters; was burned again, in 1481, by an English fleet; was the meeting place, in 1488, of James III, and his rebellious nobles for effecting a pacification; witnessed, in 1547, the burning or capture, by an English admiral, of ten vessels which had anchored near it for protection; was garrisoned, in 1548, during the regency of the Earl of Arran, by a French force under D'Esse; underwent repeated vicissitudes of occupancy till 1572; served, like the Bass, as a State prison for confining distinguished Covenanters in the time of the persecution; and was one of the chief forts of Scotland guaranteed by the Act of Union to be maintained permanently as a national strength.

> It is in the care of Historic Scotland; open Apr-Sep daily and Oct-Mar Sat-Wed. Tel 01506 834807.

Blackness Castle

5 /Mannerston (*)

Ordnance Survey (OSR) = NT 048790

Return on the B903 for 0.75 miles, then turn left signed A904 to Edinburgh. Just before the second left turn Mannerston is on the right, surrounded by a low wall.

Structure

Mannerston is a much-altered late 17th-century house, originally L-shaped on plan and two storeys and a garret in height. The masonry is rubble. The window margins are back-set, and the gables are crow-stepped.

History

Mannerston is part of the barony of Abercorn, from which the Dukes of Abercorn take their title. The earliest date found is of Henry Livingston of Mannerston in 1431. He had at least two sons, Henry and Robert, of whom Henry succeeded to Mannerston. The Livingstons of Mannerston were kin to the family of Livingston of Callendar, and thus kinsmen to the Livingston Earls of Linlithgow and Newburgh.

Edward Bruce, second son of Sir Robert Bruce of Clackmannan, married Agnes, one of three daughters and co-heiresses of William Airth of that ilk and widow of Livingston of Mannerston. With her came the lands and barony of Airth, and this became Edward's chief title afterwards.

The property can be viewed from the road.

Mannerston

6 The Binns (*)

Ordnance Survey (OSR) = NT 051785

> Continue on this minor road to the A904. Turn left and immediate left into the grounds of The Binns.

Structure

The southern part of the present east wing of the Binns may represent the original structure. Dalyell began to build a new house some time before 1621, and completed it by 1630. This seemed to be the north-western portion of the present entrance front, an oblong block of originally three storeys and a garret, and having two turnpike turrets set symmetrically on the north side. There were four main chambers, all unvaulted, on each floor.

Brief History

For more than four centuries it has been the seat of a branch of the Dalyells. The Binns was the birthplace of Sir Thomas Dalyell (1599-1685), the bearded Muscovy general, who routed the Covenanters at Rullion Green in 1666; who, in old age, adorned this mansion with fine gardens; and who, in 1681, embodied here the Scots Greys regiment. In 1685 his son received a baronetcy, whose sixth holder, Sir John Graham Dalyell (1776-1851), was an eminent antiquary, and author of 17 works.

> It is in the care of The National Trust for Scotland; house open June-September, Saturday-Thursday; parkland open all year around. Tel 01506 834255.

The Binns

7 Midhope Castle (*)

Ordnance Survey (OSR) = NT 073787

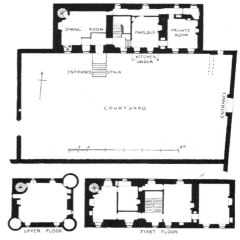

Return to the A904 and turn left. After 2 miles, signed Abercorn, turn left, and left again after 0.75 miles into the private road

Structure

It is a house of the 16th century, with the approach from the east over the burn, just beyond which lay the entrance with two Renaissance gate-piers of late 17th- or early 18th-century type. The house had been extended in a wing to the east and formed the northern side of a courtyard, which was entered from the east through an ashlared gateway. The upper part had apparently been rebuilt with chambers, all unvaulted, on each floor. The tower was lofty, having a vaulted basement, three upper floors, and an attic and garret. It was oblong on plan, and the masonry was rubble brought to courses. At three angles two-storeyed turrets were corbelled out.

Brief History

There were a father and son, his successor, of the same name, the latter being dead by 1619. Alexander Drummond of Midhope

Midhope Castle – plan

was in trouble politically in 1571. Sir Robert Drummond of Midhope lived after the Restoration of King Charles II.

The Castle is being restored and on a private road.

Midhope Castle

8 Staneyhill Tower (*)

Ordnance Survey (OSR) = NT 092784

Return to the A904 and turn left and drive for 2.5 miles. Turn left signed Hopetoun House, and having turned left under the bridge follow the signs to the House.

Staneyhill Tower

Structure

Until recently it was a fragment of a 17th-century house built on the traditional L-plan. The re-entrant lies open to the south-east and contained an octagonal stair-tower of unusual size, which stood complete to its terminal, a parapeted look-out. The other parts of the house were reduced to the vaults covering the basement floor. There had been two upper storeys. The masonry of the building was rubble with quoins.

The ruin is located in the Deer Park within the grounds of Hopetoun House. Anyone wishing to see the tower must make prior contact with the Estate office, because access could be denied for health and safety reasons. No dogs are allowed. Details of Hopetoun House can be found on page 201.

Staneyhill Tower

9 *Duntarvie Castle (*)*

Ordnance Survey (OSR) = NT 091765

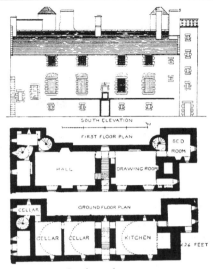

SOUTH ELEVATION

FIRST FLOOR PLAN

HALL   DRAWING ROOM   BED ROOM

GROUND FLOOR PLAN

CELLAR   CELLAR   CELLAR   KITCHEN   24 FEET

Duntarvie Castle – plans

Retrace your steps on the A904 back almost to Staneyhill Tower, but then turn left on the B8020 to Winchburgh. Duntarvie is on the right after 0.75 miles.

Structure

The old mansion dates from the end of the 16th century, and is currently undergoing restoration, although still roofless. It comprised an oblong block, four storeys in height, with square towers of five storeys attached to its northern angles; in the northern re-entrants thus formed, circular stair-turrets were corbelled out and rose above the main roof to give access to the balustraded look-outs formed on the flat roofs of the towers. The entrance was centred in the south front and opened on the main staircase. The masonry was rubble and was probably harled. The windows were chamfered

Brief History

Duntarvie was for nearly two centuries a seat of the Durhams. James Durham of Duntarvie is on record in 1588.

The Castle is being restored and can be seen from the road.

Duntarvie Castle

10 Niddry Castle (*)

Ordnance Survey (OSR) = NT 097743

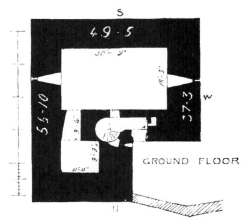

Niddry Castle – plan

Continue on the road to Winchburgh. At the junction turn right on the B9080 (Linlithgow), and then left signed Niddry Castle. After 0.75 miles turn left, pass over two bridges and then turn left into the entry lane to the castle.

Structure

Niddry dates from the end of the 15th century or beginning of the 16th. It is built on the L-shaped plan, the re-entrant angle opening to the north-west, and lay partly if not wholly within the barmkin. The top storey above the parapet is a reconstruction possibly of the 17th century. Between the windows were cannon-shaped spouts. The main walling was rubble, built in stretchers with pinnings, and the dressings were of freestone; the windows were chamfered. Below the wall head there were four storeys in the tower, and above that level one storey and perhaps a loft.

Brief History

It was here that Lord Seton conducted Queen Mary on the night of her escape from Lochleven Castle, 2nd May 1568. From Niddry she sent a messenger to ask assistance from the court of England, and next day she rode on to the Hamiltons.

It was built by George, 4th Lord Seton, who

Niddry Castle

fell at Flodden, and remained in possession of the Seton family until the reign of Charles II, when the lands came into possession of the Hopes, ancestors of the Earls of Hopetoun. Sir Richard Maitland said that George, 6th Lord Seton, who succeeded in 1545, "repairlit and biggit ane grit part of the hous and place of West Nethrie".

There is a public footpath running to the back of the castle, and passing through the garden to the east of the castle, so the owners would appreciate adherence to footpath. The owners are members of the Scottish Castles Association, and the Events Programme may include Niddry Castle from time to time.

11 Illieston House (*)

Ordnance Survey (OSR) = NT 010700

Out of Niddry turn left and veer right and drive for 1.5 miles. At the junction turn right on the A89, and just before the roundabout turn left to Kilpunt. Turn right at the next junction and then left to Muirend. Go round the bend in Muirend and take the first left down the track to Illieston.

Structure

A corruption of Elliston, it is an interesting 17th-century house, whose approach is from the north-west, where a short, straight avenue led to a forecourt flanked by oblong crow-stepped office-buildings, stable, coach-house, and dairy. It was three storeys in height and was rectangular on plan, with a projecting stair-tower on the south, having a turret-stair corbelled out in the eastern re-entrant angle to give access to a chamber on the top storey. The ground floor was vaulted and had at the north-east angle a service newel-stair rising to the first floor of the main building. The masonry was rubble with polished dressings rounded at jamb and lintel, and was keyed for harling.

Brief History

In 1255, Ralph Noble resigned Illieston in the hands of his brother Thomas, who granted a charter of the lands to Sir David de Graham. The lands remained with the Grahams until 1539, when William, 3rd Earl of Menteith gave the estate to his brother-in-law, James Hamilton, Earl of Arran. James II and James IV are said to have used Illieston, as a hunting seat and, considering the close links with the Hamiltons, this seems not improbable.

John Ellis purchased Illieston in 1664, an Edinburgh advocate. He built the present castle which today is the oldest continuously inhabited building in the parish. The initials MIE (Master John Ellis) can be seen on the entrance gate is dated 1665. Illieston returned to the Hamiltons in 1693 when purchased by Lord John Hamilton, fourth son of William and Anne, Duke and Duchess of Hamilton. They sold it to the Earl of Hopetoun in 1765, and it belonged to the Hopetoun Estate until 1950, when it was purchased by the tenant, Stewart Brownlie, dairy farmer, whose family are still in possession.

It is a private residence, but can be seen from the lane.

Illieston Castle

12 Houstoun House (*)

Ordnance Survey (OSR) = NT 058716

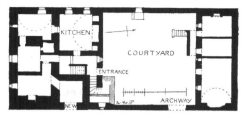

Houston House – plan

Retrace your steps back to the A89 and turn left. At the roundabout take the A899 and drive through Broxburn and Uphall. Go straight through the traffic lights in Uphall and Houston House is immediately after the next mini-roundabout on the left.

Structure

The house is lofty, with several facades, harled and many-windowed. It is almost square on plan and formed the southern boundary of a small courtyard, walled at the sides and with a two-storeyed stable block on the north. As it now stands, it is a large mansion of the later 17th century, but the present south-eastern portion is earlier. It was possibly L-shaped on plan, with the re-entrant angle lying open to the north-west, and contained a newel-stair tower. The main block had been extended westward, and a wing returned northward, while a scale-stair was placed between this new wing and the old; the back door, which opened beneath the stair, is dated 1757.

Brief History

Although the Barony of Houstoun is known to have existed in the 12th century, its history is mainly linked to the Shairp family, who were lairds here for almost four centuries. The Houstoun Papers, dating from the early 15th century, are on permanent loan to the Scottish Records Office.

The first Shairp of Houstoun, Sir Thomas, acquired the estates in 1569. Though advocate to Mary Queen of Scots, he was involved in nearly 13 years of litigation before establishing his title; and only then did he begin to build his new mansion.

The property is now a well-established 4 star Country House Hotel.

In principle the hotel does not have any objections to visitors, but there will be restrictions when there are weddings and events in the grounds. A telephone call before hand would be welcome. Tel 01506 853831.

Houston House

13 Ochiltree Castle

Ordnance Survey (OSR) = NT 032748

> Return to the traffic lights in Uphall and turn left on the B8046. After 1.75 miles turn left signed Ochiltree. The castle is on the right after a further 2 miles.

Structure

Ochiltree is an L-shaped tower house with a turnpike stair in the re-entrant angle facing north east. The main part of the building dates to the first part of the 16th century, but there is no record of the details of its building. It is a four storeyed tower with two bartizans. They are unusual in that they are of different sizes, the north west one being on the third floor, while the south east one is entered from the bedroom on the second floor. Both functioned as garderobes. The house was modified and extended significantly when the fortunes of the Stirling family were supplemented by the marriage in 1589 of Sir Archibald Stirling of Keir to Dame Grisel Ross. The principal alterations were the

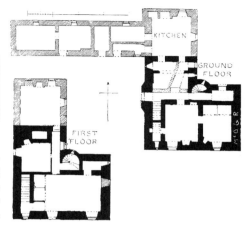

Ochiltree Castle – plans

building of the north wing, the straight staircase to the great hall and the doors facing north and west.

Brief History

The lands of Ochiltree are mentioned in records dating back to the 11th century. The first recorded owner was Thorold, who was a Norman knight allocated the lands of

Ochiltree Castle

Ochiltree in 1086 by Malcolm Canmore. Thorold was depicted on the Bayeux Tapestry as the dwarf swinging on the reigns of two knights' horses. It is believed that his family, variously known as De Strivelyn, Skirving and Stirling for the next 500 years, owned the lands. Their descendants still own the lands of Keir near Stirling.

In the 15th century, Prince David came wooing a daughter of the de Strivelyn household. Although they did not wed, they had a child Michael of Ochiltree (1409-1477), who became Bishop of Dunblane. In 1437 Michael was asked to anoint and crown his nephew, James II, who was only six years of age at the time.

> The owners are members of the Scottish Castles Association, and the Events Programme may include Ochiltree Castle from time to time.

Ochiltree Castle

14 Calder House (*)

Ordnance Survey (OSR) = NT 073673

Turn left signed Dechmont, and at the next junction turn left again to West Binny. Continue into Dechmont and at that junction turn left and then right on the A899. Follow the A899 to Livingston. Take the first left at Lizzie Brice's roundabout, go through the village and turn right at the Black Bull. The entrance to the House is on the right.

Calder House

Structure

Calder is a 17th-century mansion, and save for modern additions, was L-shaped on plan, the re-entrant angle being open to the north. The house was four storeys high to the wall-head, but at the extremity of the wing there were five storeys. The masonry was rough-cast and was built of rubble, in small stones, uncoursed, in the original work, and in large stones roughly cubical and brought to courses in the addition; the voids had dressed and back-set margins, and the quoins were rusticated. Within the main block were three contiguous vaulted chambers with an unvaulted one at the east end.

Brief History

This seat is famous for the celebration of the Lord's Supper in its great hall by John Knox in 1556. For more than five centuries it was a seat of the Sandilands.

It is a private residence, and therefore permission should be sought before entry into the grounds.

Calder House

15 Alderstone House

Ordnance Survey (OSR) = NT 044662

Continue on the road to the junction and turn left on the B8046 and return to the roundabout. Straight across on the A71, and then turn right at the roundabout signed Almondvale. At the third roundabout turn left into Alderstone Business Park. First roundabout pass Konica Minolta take the first left and then first right into MacMillan Road where the premises are situated.

Structure

It is a plain altered 16th-century L-shaped tower house of three storeys, rectangular in plan. It has two wings on either side of the newel turnpike stair. It was extended in the 17th century. The basement is vaulted, and contained the kitchen with a wide fireplace.

Brief History

The Kinloch family purchased the Alderstone estate in 1556 and the house was built by advocate Patrick Kinloch. In 1656 was acquired by the Sandilands Lord Torphichen, who sold it to John Mitchell of Todhaugh in 1692. In the 19th century it passed to the Bruce family, and then in the 20th century the Whitelaw family, of whom former Secretary of State, Viscount Willie Whitelaw, is the most famous member, purchased it.

It is currently used as company offices, and visitors should make themselves known at reception.

Alderstone House

16 Murieston Castle (*)

Ordnance Survey (OSR) = NT 050636

Turn right out of MacMillan Road and right again at the junction, and at the Campus roundabout turn right back to wards the A71. At the next roundabout on the A71 (Wilderness) turn left and left again at the mini-roundabout and over the railway line. Take the second right, on the bend, and keep right driving down the lane to Murieston Farm.

Structure

This is the ruin of a freestanding 16th-century tower that was drastically restored around 1836. A portion of a semi-circular turret, projecting at first floor level from the south wall and borne on moulded corbelling of the 16th century, was the only feature that had survived.

Brief History

In February 1559 John Sandilands, feuar of Calder, set the lands of Wester Muirstone with others to James Cochrane, his servitor.

The ruin is within a farm, but the owners readily accept visitors providing they ask permission beforehand.

Murieston Castle

17 Linnhouse (*)

Ordnance Survey (OSR) = NT 062630

Return to the main road and turn right, then right again into Castleview Lane. Pass under the bridge and Linnhouse is signed on the left.

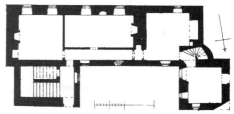

Linnhouse – plan

Structure

The structure from the end of the 16th century is of two periods. The earlier part was built in 1589 on a variant of the L-plan and comprised two wings, rectangularly disposed and attached at one angle only. Towards the close of the 17th century, or in the early 18th century, a considerable L-planned addition was made to the east, converting the whole into a hollow square on plan. Both nucleus and extension were three storeys in height and had crow-stepped gables.

Brief History

The property of Linnhouse belonged in the 16th century to the Tennents, one of whom, James Tennent of Lynhouse, was witness in a charter of James, Lord of St John, preceptor of Torphichen, Knight of the Order of St John of Jerusalem, to Gavin Dundas of Brestmill, in 1588. Some of the family seem to have been burgesses of Edinburgh, and one was Provost in 1571, and was taken prisoner while fighting for Queen Mary. This connection may perhaps account for the motto of Edinburgh being inscribed over the doorway.

It is a private residence, and therefore permission should be sought before entering the grounds.

Linnhouse

18 Cairns Castle (*)

Ordnance Survey (OSR) = NT 091604

Retrace your steps and take first left after the bridge. After 1.5 miles turn left to Carnwath, and then after a further 2.5 miles turn left on the A70 (Edinburgh). Another 2.5 miles of driving before turning right on a bend with a reservoir on the right. Park in the car park before the private road. The castle is 400 yards down the road.

Structure

Cairns is a ruined 15th-century tower, which on plan the structure comprised a rectangular tower, and to it attached a wing which projected southward from the lateral wall, and show that there were at least three storeys beneath the wall-head. The basement of both portions was vaulted and there were two entrances, both in the east wall.

Brief History

The Crichtons owned the lands of Cairns at least early in the 15th century until around the middle of the following century. In 1542 there is a confirmation of transference of the lands of Easter Cairns with the tower to John Tennent, and in this family they remained for another 150 years.

The ruin can be viewed from the car park.

Cairns Castle

19 Bedlormie (*)

Ordnance Survey (OSR) = NT 874675

Return to the A70 and turn left. It is a long journey to Bedlormie. 2.5 miles to the right turn on the B7008 and then drive to West Calder. Turn left and then right on the B792. In Blackburn turn left at the junction on to the A705. Go through Whitburn, turn right and then left on to the B7066 to Harthill. Turn right on the B718 to Blackridge and then after 1.75 miles turn left on the A89. Bedlormie is on the left after 1 mile.

Structure

It is a small harled house built on an L-plan and dating from the 17th century, but has been reduced in height to two storeys and considerably altered; the re-entrant angle opens to the north-west and contains the newel-stair within a circular tower. The lower windows of the house had a roll-and-quirk moulding on jambs and lintel, while the upper windows had margins back-set and chamfered. Neither storey is vaulted, and internally the structure has been modernised. The parlour which faces south, contained figures, scroll-work, and a cartouche.

Brief History

In 1424 John de "Murrefe" of Ogilface granted the whole lands of Bedlormie to Sir John "Forstare", Master of the King's Household. In 1645 George, Lord Forrester of Corstorphine, was superior of Bedlormie, and the lands were held from him by Patrick Walker. It came by marriage, in the 17th century, to the baronet family of Livingstone.

It is a private residence; therefore permission should be sought before entering the grounds.

Bedlormie

20 Bridge Castle (*)

Ordnance Survey (OSR) = NT 944709

Return on the A89 through Blackridge to Armadale, and turn left on the B8084. Turn left at the end of the village, just before the Golf Club. Turn right at the junction, and Bridge Castle is 0.75 miles on the left behind the trees.

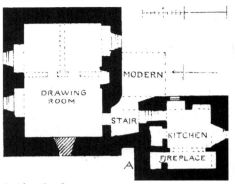

Bridge Castle

Structure

The northern portion has been a tower dating from the 16th century, L-shaped on plan and containing three storeys and attics. To this has been added a wing, four storeys and an attic in height, linked for convenience to the original wing, which contained the staircase. It was built of rubble with dressed quoins. Most of the windows have been altered, but those which are original have a quirked edge-roll on jamb and lintel. It seems to have been rebuilt in the 17th century, but before the wing was added. The later wing has no parapet. The main block is vaulted on the ground floor.

Brief History

The property passed into the possession of Livingston, Earl of Linlithgow, in 1588, when James VI conferred the charter.

The property can be seen from the road.

Bridge Castle

21 *Couston Castle (*)*

Ordnance Survey (OSR) = NT 955712

Turn right at the next junction. At the next junction with the A801 turn left and immediately right. Couston Farm is down the second left turn and the ruins are part of the farm.

Structure

Lying on the east side of the farmhouse of North Couston are the fragmentary remains of the castle, which date from the 17th century. On plan the building has been L-shaped. The wing, in which lies the entrance, projected on the north-west and evidently contained the newel stair. The masonry is rubble, irregularly coursed and pinned. The entrance bears a bold quirked edge-roll, the basement windows that remain are chamfered, and one of the first-floor windows had a moulded scontion. At basement level there were two chambers in the main block. The smaller, which lay at the eastern end, had been a vaulted cellar; the larger was the kitchen and retained the fireplace arch in the west gable, but no trace of the vault remains.

Please seek permission from the farm.

Couston Castle

22 Kipps Castle (*)

Ordnance Survey (OSR) = NT 989739

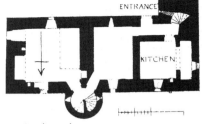

Kipps Castle – plan

From Couston Castle return to the main road (A800); turn right (west) and drive a short distance to T-junction with A801. Turn right and drive north for 1 mile to roundabout. Turn right (east) on to B8047. At junction after 2.5 miles, on outskirts of Torphichen, cross straight ahead on to unclassified road. Continue east and then north for 2 miles, when a track on left side of road, leading to Kipps and Kipps Farm, is seen on left. Stay on the road for some 300 to 400 yards until a public car park is found on the left (west) side of the road. Park and continue on foot, following signposts for public footpath to Cockleroy; once you are on the open hillside, the ruin of Kipps can be seen to the left (the south), across a small valley. There are the remains of a hill fort at the summit of Cockleroy.

Structure

On plan the ruin of Kipps is an oblong block, with a rectangular stair-tower at the south-western angle and a circular stair-tower projecting from the north wall. The western portion including the stairs seems to have been the original house, which was being built around 1625. The structure has been three storeys. The masonry was of rubble with dressed quoins, and originally was harled. The entrance opened on a small lobby giving access to the south-west stair and two vaulted chambers.

Brief History

Tombs of the Boyds of Kipps are in the church of the Preceptory at Torphichen. Robert Boyd of Kipps, advocate, died in 1645, leaving only daughters. One daughter married David Sibbald, and their third son, Sir Robert Sibbald, physician, naturalist and antiquary, who died in 1722, lived at Kipps for many years.

The ruins can be seen from the road.

Kipps Castle

23 Torphichen Preceptory (*)

Ordnance Survey (OSR) = NT 972727

Return to the main road and turn right into Torphichen. Turn right in the village for the Preceptory. The Torphichen Inn is worth a visit.

Structure

All that has survived is the crossing and transepts of the church surmounted respectively by a bell-tower and upper chambers. The parish church, a late 17th-century structure, occupied the site of the nave. The precinct had evidently been walled extending from Bowgate to the remains of a circular tower in the manse garden. Externally the masonry was ashlar work wrought from a local freestone; the interior of crossing, tower, and transepts and the vaulting were also of ashlar, but the upper chambers were merely ashlar-faced with rubble work behind.

Brief History

Torphichen Preceptory was the main seat of the Knights Hospitallers from the 12th century. William Wallace held a convention of barons here in 1298, and Edward I of England stayed here after winning the Battle of Falkirk against Wallace the same year.

It is in the care of Historic Scotland. Preceptory and parish church open Apr-Sep, Sat 11.00-17.00, Sun and Bank Hols 14.00-17.00: tel 01506 653475.

Torphichen Preceptory

24 Lochcote Castle (*)

Ordnance Survey (OSR) = NT 976737

Continue on the minor road, which is a right turn out of the Preceptory, and drive downhill to a right turn to Craigend. The ruin is a 0.75 mile walk from there.

Structure

Only a fragment remains of this 17th–century building, which consisted of a small vaulted chamber, probably the remains of an angle tower, with a window in each wall. It was built of rubble with rounded external corners, the southern being corbelled out to the square.

Brief History

It was a property of the Crawfords.

Assistance should be sought from the farm steading.

Lochcote Castle

25 Carriber Castle (*)

Ordnance Survey (OSR) = NT 966751

Return to Torphichen and drive north on the B792 and then turn left on the A706. Take the first right and right again at the junction. After 1.5 miles at the roundabout turn right on the B825 to Linlithgow. After 0.75 miles turn right into Muiravonside Country Park. Seek assistance for the location of the ruins.

Structure

The fragmentary remains of this house stand on the right bank of the steep Carriber Glen.

At the northern end there seemed to have been a square courtyard with an oblong block on the northern and southern sides. The only feature was a chamfered doorway in the western wall, which seemed no earlier than the 17th century. South of the courtyard there has been an oblong range, probably stabling or byres. The remaining walls were built of rubble.

Brief History

Robert Gib of Carribers was the Queen's principal Bailie of the port of Newhaven in 1553.

Freely accessible within the Country Park.

© Reproduced by kind permission of John Pringle

Carriber Castle

26 Inveravon Castle (*)

Ordnance Survey (OSR) = NT 953798

Turn left out of the country park and then right at the roundabout. After 2.5 miles pass over the motorway and follow minor road passing the Golf Club and Dry Ski Slope to Old Polmont. At junction turn right over the bridge on to the B904. Turn right to Inveravon, climb uphill and the tower is on the left just before the wall.

Structure

It is a fragment of the outer semi-circle of the tower. It was built of sandstone rubble in laid courses. Within was the basement, vaulted with a segmental arch with access from a door on the west. It is apparently a 15th century work, as the record of its destruction by James II indicated.

Brief History

The castle, mentioned in the Auchinleck chronicle of James II, is supposed to have occupied the site of the Roman station; and the ruin which stands here may have been one of the corner towers of that castle.

Can be seen from the road.

Inveravon Castle

27 Kinneil House (*)

Ordnance Survey (OSR) = NT 983806

Return to the B904 and turn right. Drive for about 2.5 miles and turn right after the Kinneil Bowling Club, and it is the first right into Kinneil Museum. Exit and turn right and then right on the A706 to Linlithgow.

Structure

The house, although it was symmetrically laid out, was a composite structure, for the present disposition dates only from the last quarter of the 17th century, when extensive alterations were undertaken by William, 3rd Duke of Hamilton, and his Duchess, Anne. As the result of extensions the house then comprised on plan a central main block rising five storeys above the forecourt, with pavilions at either side, a storey lower, and stair-towers set at the back in the western re-entrant angles. On the north there was a wing, three-storeyed, having a northward return.

Brief History

It was plundered and burned by Queen Mary's opponents in 1568-70. In the reign of King Charles II, Duchess Anne and Duke William altered it. Dugald Stewart last tenanted it from 1809 till shortly before his death in 1828.

It is freely accessible to view from outside.

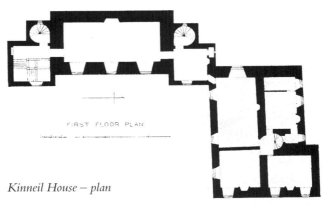

FIRST FLOOR PLAN

Kinneil House – plan

Kinneil House

Castle Touring Guides

Additional Information

Arniston House

The entrance to Arniston is on the B6372 one mile to the west of its junction with the A7 road from Edinburgh to Galashiels. The junction is near the village of Gorebridge and is sign-posted to Temple.

Arniston has been the home of the Dundas family for over four hundred years. The present owners, direct descendants of the first occupants, take pride in opening their home with its wonderful architecture, and period contents.

Arniston is situated almost due south of Edinburgh about eleven miles from the city centre. Although so close to the city, the house is set in a tranquil policies surrounded by farmland and forest.

The mansion house you see today was begun in 1726 and completed in the 1750s on the site of a previous tower house. The architect was William Adam but his son John, brother of the more famous Robert,

Arniston House

completed the building. Between them, the brothers designed and built many great Scottish buildings including the New Town of Edinburgh.

The Dundases of Arniston were, through the generations, a successful family and in the 1700s were one of the most powerful families in Scotland, the legal profession being the principal field of achievement. Solicitor General, Lord Advocate for Scotland and Lord President of the Court of Session being some of the family's appointments.

Many of the family had their portraits painted by contemporary artists including Henry Raeburn and Allan Ramsay. These and other pictures now hang at Arniston and form a fine collection, including one of Robert Dundas, 3rd Lord Arniston, 1685-1753, who was Lord President of the Court of Session.

As well as the paintings, there is to be admired the magnificent Adam architecture with moulded ceilings, fireplaces, stucco work and a collection of fine furniture and other fascinating contents.

The west side of the house was ravaged by dry rot, discovered in the 1950s. This required the gutting of the wing, which included the John Adam Dining Room and Drawing Room.

These rooms have now been faithfully restored, with grant aid from Historic Scotland, and their completion returns the house to the elegant and comfortable family dwelling it was and is today.

In April, May and June the house is open to the public every Tuesday and Wednesday for guided tours, starting at 2 pm and 3.30 pm. These take about an hour to complete. From July to 11th September the house is open for guided tours on every day of the week except Saturdays starting at 2 pm and 3.30 pm. The grounds are open from 2pm till 5pm. The family are involved as much as possible in the showing of the house and recounting the history. Well-informed guides assist them. Outwith these dates parties of between 10 and 50 are welcomed by prior arrangement. Entry to the house is by tour only. For pre-arranged visits please contact:
Mail: The Administrator Henrietta Dundas-Bekker, Arniston House, Gorebridge, Midlothian, EH23 4RY.
Tel: +44 (0) 1875 830 515
Fax: +44 (0) 1875 830 515.
Email: arnistonhouse@btconnect.com
Web: www.arniston-house.co.uk

Newhailes

Structure and History

In a landscaped and wooded park with good views over the Forth, Newhailes is a plain and austere symmetrical mansion. It was first built in 1686 by the architect James Smith; and there are fine rococo interiors, including the library, and a good collection of pictures and portraits. The mansion was extended about 1750.

The property was once known as Whitehill, but, when it was purchased by the Dalrymples, the name was changed to Newhailes, from their estate of Hailes near East Linton in East Lothian. Newhailes was visited by many of the luminaries of the Scottish Enlightenment but is now in the care of The National Trust for Scotland.

Newhailes is on the A6095 to the south and west of Musselburgh. It is open at Easter, and then from May to September for guided tours. There is a visitor centre and tearoom, as well as a plant centre. There is an admission charge to get into the house. Tel: 0131 665 1546.

Dalmeny House

Structure

When Dalmeny House was completed in 1817, it marked a great departure in Scottish architecture; its Tudor Gothic style, with its highly decorated chimneys and crenellations, looked back toward fanciful 16th-century English mansions, such as Hampton Court. The house was designed by a University friend of the 4th Earl of Rosebery, William Wilkins, who would go on to design the National Gallery in London and much of King's College, Cambridge - parts of which closely resemble Dalmeny.

With its Gothic Great Hall and corridor, its large, formal regency apartments and its sweeping views across the Firth of Forth, it is a house which combines comfort and romanticism, and which produced many imitations throughout Scotland.

As one wanders through the house, each room opens up a new experience, highlighting different parts of the remarkable collection of art and objects. Yet Dalmeny House preserves the overall feeling of the family home it still is.

History

The family name of the Earls of Rosebery is Primrose, a name associated with lands in Fife owned by Dunfermline Abbey. The earliest known member of the family, Henry, was born in 1490; his grandson James became Clerk to the Privy Council under James the VI and I and died in 1640.

James' son, Archibald Primrose, succeeded his father as Clerk to the Privy Council during the perilous period leading up to the Civil War. Praised by Charles I for his "fidelity, judgement and discretion", he fought on the Royalist side, lost his estates and, at one point, was under sentence of death. His capable and unswerving service to the exiled Stuart kings earned him a knighthood at the Restoration and appointment as Lord Clerk Register of Scotland. In 1662, he bought the Barony of Barnbougle and Dalmeny and moved into the 13th-century tower house on the shore.

His youngest son, also Archibald, fought with the Imperial Army in Hungary during the reign of James VII. On the 1st April 1700 he was raised to the peerage as Viscount Rosebery, a title he took from Rosebery Topping, a hill near his wife's estate in Yorkshire. He was made Earl of Rosebery in 1703 in Queen Anne's Coronation Honours.

There have been seven earls of Rosebery and ten countesses, three of the earls having married twice. The eldest son of the Earl of Rosebery usually takes the courtesy title of Viscount Dalmeny.

Dalmeny House, family home of the Earls of Rosebery, is set in parkland overlooking the Firth of Forth, just west of Edinburgh, off the A90. It is open to the public from 2pm to 5:30pm Sunday, Monday and Tuesday afternoons in July and August. There are guided tours and a tearoom serving light refreshments. Outside these times, guided tours, with optional refreshments, are available to groups by prior arrangement. Last admission is 4.30pm. Tel 0131 331 1888 or web www.dalmeny.co.uk

ℋopetoun ℋouse

Structure

Hopetoun House is one of the most splendid examples of Georgian architecture in Britain being the work of Scottish architects Sir William Bruce and William Adam.

Work on the house began in 1699 under the auspices of Sir William Bruce, were completed in 1707, and produced some of the finest examples of carving, wainscoting and ceiling painting in Scotland. Many details, such as the grand staircase, were executed by local craftsmen such as Alexander Eizat who had worked with Bruce during renovations at Holyrood Palace in Edinburgh.

Some fourteen years later in 1721, the renowned Scottish architect, William Adam, was commissioned to undertake a programme of alterations and improvements that lasted until 1767. This saw the enlargement of the house by the addition of an imposing facade with magnificent colonnades, north and south pavilions and the creation of grand state apartments to be used for entertaining and socialising. The work outlived William Adam, however, and after his death in 1748 his sons

John and Robert carried out the interior decoration of the house. The work also outlived the 1st Earl: his son John, the 2nd Earl, (1704–1781) oversaw the completion of the interiors.

Since its completion in the mid 18th century, the house has remained substantially unaltered save for the 4th Earl's internal modifications between 1816 and 1823, including the creation of the Large and Small Libraries and the decoration of the State Dining Room by James Gillespie Graham.

History

Hopetoun has been the home of the Earls of Hopetoun, later created Marquesses of Linlithgow, since it was built in 1699 and part of the House is still lived in today by the present Marquess and his family.

The family origins are generally believed to date back to a John Hope, shown in the Edinburgh Burgess Rolls of 1516–1517 with the alias Petit Johnne, Trumpetour. John's son Henry (circa 1533–1591) was a burgess both of Dieppe and of Edinburgh and his son, Sir Thomas Hope of Craighall (1573–1646), was appointed King's Advocate by Charles I in 1626. Sir Thomas' fourth son, Sir James Hope

Hopetoun House

(1614-1661) was the first to style himself 'of Hopetoun' using the old name for Leadhills in Lanarkshire where, through his marriage with the heiress Anne Foulis, he came into possession of valuable lead mines.

James the 3rd Earl (1741-1816) had no son, so he was succeeded by his half-brother General Sir John Hope (1765-1823) as 4th Earl. He was the Captain General of the Royal Company of Archers. The 5th Earl was active in Scottish affairs and in the continued improvements of his estates. The 6th Earl died of typhoid at the age of 42 after a brief life devoted to Paris and the Pytchley Hunt. The 7th Earl, John (1860-1908), however, was to become one of the most eminent members of the family and was created the 1st Marquess of Linlithgow. After serving as Governor of Victoria, Australia at the age of 29, he returned to Britain to become Queen Victoria's Lord Chamberlain. He went back as the first Governor General of the newly-formed Commonwealth of Australia in 1900. He was also Secretary for Scotland in Arthur Balfour's Government of 1905.

His son Victor, 8th Earl and 2nd Marquess (1887-1952), eclipsed even these great achievements. He was civil Lord of the Admiralty from 1922 to 1924; chaired the Royal Commission on Agriculture in India (1926-1928). In 1928 he was made a Knight of the Order of the Thistle. He chaired the committee on Indian constitutional reform in 1933 and helped formulate the Government of India Act of 1935. Following his experience in India he returned there as Viceroy and Governor General from 1936 to 1943, almost two full terms of office, making him the longest-serving Viceroy. For this he was created a Knight of the Order of the Garter, one of only a handful of non-royals to be a Knight both of the Garter and of the Thistle.

Charles, 9th Earl and 3rd Marquess (1912-1987) served in the Second World War and was taken prisoner with the 51st (Highland) Division in 1940 before being held at Colditz. He and his son Adrian, the present Marquess, were responsible for the formation of the Hopetoun House Preservation Trust in 1974. The present Marquess continues to live in the House, and he and his son Andrew, Earl of Hopetoun are both active members of the Board of Trustees.

Off the A904 2.5 miles west of Edinburgh, the House and Grounds are open to the public daily from Easter to the end of September but pre-booked group visits can be accommodated throughout the year. Hopetoun is also available for weddings and all types of corporate hospitality. The Stables Tearoom offers wonderful lunches and tempting snacks with champagne afternoon teas a speciality. Tel 0131 331 2451 or web www.hopetounhouse.com

Newliston

Structure

The fine and tall classical mansion was built by the architect Robert Adam in 1789 on the site of an old tower house. It was extended in the middle of the 19th century; and there is a walled garden, as well as an old doocot which has been converted into a house.

History

The lands were owned by the Dundas family until 1699 when they went to the Dalrymples of Stair, then later to the Hogs, whose descendants still own the property.

Newliston is about 1 mile southwest of Kirkliston off the A89. It is open from May to the beginning of June. There is a tearoom and admission charge. Tel: 0131 331 3231.

Melville Castle

Structure

The story behind Melville Castle is like a fairy tale come true. Ten years ago this magnificent baronial mansion house, built in 1786 for the first Viscount Melville and designed by the renowned architect James Playfair, had been left unoccupied for some time and allowed to become virtually derelict. This was indeed a tragedy for an A-listed building described as of "outstanding architectural and historic significance". The Hay family came to its rescue, purchased the property and over the past five years have completely restored it into a luxurious and stylish country-house hotel. The castle is set in a secluded situation on the bank of the North Esk River within a fifty-acre wooded estate.

Melville Castle – before restoration

family residents still lurk in the castle today. The new proprietor William Hay and others have seen the ghost of Elizabeth Rennie, wife of Henry Dundas (or Mary, Queen of Scots), during the restoration. He witnessed the apparition glide through a solid wall in the castle and during later renovations an old blocked off doorway was found where she disappeared.

History

Henry Dundas commissioned it. In earlier days, Mary, Queen of Scots, used it as a hunting lodge, while her courtiers lived nearby in the area still today called Little France. In the 19th century, Queen Victoria came to visit, as well as George IV and the novelist Sir Walter Scott. It is said that former

The Hotel welcomes the discerning guest and also specialises in Wedding Receptions, Conferences and Corporate Events.
Tel:+44 ()131 654 0088
Fax:+44 (0)131 654 4666.
Email: reception@melvillecastle.com
Web: www.melvillecastle.com

Melville Castle – today

Index of Castles

Further Reading

The Castellated & Domestic Architecture of Scotland (5 vols). Macgibbon & Ross. The definitive works.

Discovering Scottish Castles (M Salter). A gazetteer of 1026 castles

The Castles of Scotland. (M Coventry) A comprehensive reference and gazetteer to more than 3000 castles and sites (fourth edition in preparation)

The Fortified House in Scotland (N Tranter). (5 vols)

The Castles of Scotland (M Salter) (5 vols)

The Castles of Glasgow and the Clyde (G W Mason)

Linlithgow

General Information

An ancient and royal burgh of West Lothian, Linlithgow lies between the Union Canal, to the south, and the M9 motorway, to the north, 18 miles west of Edinburgh. A Roman fort and later a castle occupied the site which was, for three centuries, an important centre of the Anglians of West Lothian. Chartered by David I in the early 12th century, it was later the seat of a sheriffdom and developed important links with church and state during the Middle Ages, particularly from the 14th century, when it was re-chartered.

The importance of the Palace greatly diminished after the Union, when James VI left for England. In 1640 Cromwell occupied the town, and he fortified the palace. The Scots Parliament continued to meet there, the last time being in 1646.

Though much has been swept aside, some interesting domestic dwellings survive from the 16th and 17th centuries in the town's High Street. The town wellhead dates from 1720 while the 1628 Cross Well survives in the form of an 1807 replica.

Its traditions and community life are retained by annual events such as the Riding of the Marches. This ceremony dates back to the 14th century and echoes the former commercial activities of the town, which included tanning, shoemaking and linen weaving.

Tourist Information Centre – Burgh Halls, The Cross (01506 844600)

Linlithgow

Dunbar

Dunbar (© John Pringle)

General Information

Dunbar became a burgh in 1370 and a Royal Burgh on 16th August 1445, but its known history extends further back in time. Dark Age and Bronze Age remains have been found.

In the Dark Ages, the Picts laid claim to Lothian and established themselves at Dunbar.

John Muir, the man recognised as the father of the modern conservation movement, spent his early life in Dunbar. A statue designed by international sculptor, Valentin Znoba, has been erected outside the Town House on the High Street. There is also a museum in the house where he lived and a large area around the estuary of the River Tyne to the North of the town has been designated the John Muir Country Park.

Tourist Information Centre 143 High Street (01368 863353)

Dunbar

Musselburgh

Musselburgh (© John Pringle)

General Information

It was first settled by the Romans in the years following their invasion of Scotland in AD80. The bridge they built outlasted them by many centuries. It was rebuilt on the original Roman foundations some time before 1300, and in 1597 it was rebuilt again, this time with a third arch added on the east side of the river. The Old Bridge is also known as the Roman Bridge and remains in use today by pedestrians. To its north is the New Bridge built in 1806. This in turn was considerably widened in 1925.

Musselburgh has other bridges. Perhaps the oddest is the "Electric Bridge". This was a road bridge built a couple of hundred yards north of the New Bridge in the 1960s to allow the transport of the turbines to the new power station then being built at Cockenzie Once used it was offered for a nominal sum to the Town Council, who turned it down.

Other recognisable parts of Musselburgh began to take shape in the 1500s. The castle-like Tolbooth which still dominates the High Street appeared in 1590. The earlier tower incorporated at its west end seems to have been built under Dutch influence, probably at the end of the 1400s. This was one of the few buildings in Musselburgh to survive a sacking by Henry VIII's English army during the "Rough Wooing" in 1544. The late 1500s also saw the building of Pinkie House, to the south east of the High Street.

A golf course had been established to the east of the town at least as early as 1672, and many claim it was the world's first proper golf course, with Mary, Queen of Scots, an early enthusiast in the 1560s.

In 1817 horse racing came to Musselburgh Links. Since then the nine holes of the Musselburgh Old Course have been contained within the racecourse. Over the years the Old Course has been home to many golf clubs, and the Open Championship was played here six times between 1874 and 1889. Visitors are welcome, and can hire traditional balls and hickory golf clubs to get a real feel for the early days of golf.

Newhailes is to the south and west of the town – see page 199.

There is no Tourist Information Centre in the burgh.

Musselburgh

Haddington

General Information

The burgh kirk of Haddington, St Mary's, stands by the River Tyne. The tower once bore a masonry crown, but it was lost and the rest of the kirk badly damaged in the English occupation in 1548-9. The kirk remained in a partly ruined condition until the 1970s, when it was restored. It can be visited.

Haddington is full of architectural treasures. Although there is a smooth Georgian façade about a lot of the town's old centre now, there is much evidence of medieval origins.

John Knox grew up here, frequently hearing the reformer George Wishart preach.

Haddington (© John Pringle)

Jane Welsh Carlyle, wife of Thomas Carlyle, was born here in 1801, as was Samuel Smiles (1812) of 'self-help' fame.

There is no Tourist Information Centre

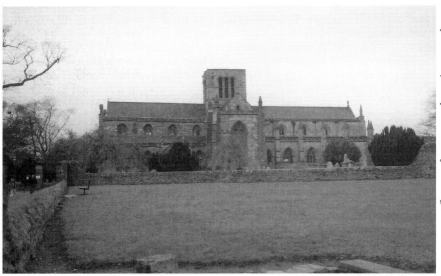

Haddington

North Berwick

General Information

North Berwick grew as a resort in the latter half of the 1800s largely because of its two sandy bays, namely Berwick Bay and Milsey Bay, but its core lies around its harbour, built into a rocky promontory projecting between the town's sandy bays. There has been a harbour of sorts in North Berwick from at least the 1100s and for the following 500 years this was the location of a ferry crossing to Earlsferry, near Elie, in Fife. A steady stream of pilgrims to St Andrews took advantage of a crossing that dramatically shortened their journey.

North Berwick Law, a volcanic rock, overlooks North Berwick to the south of the town.

Don't miss the Napoleonic signal station and an arch made from a pair of whale's jaw bones.

The Scottish Seabird Centre is an award-winning wildlife visitor centre and one of Scotland's five star attractions. From its stunning location overlooking the sea and islands of the Forth, visitors enjoy a close encounter with nature to remember.

Tourist Information Centre, Quality Street (01620 893667)

North Berwick

Dalkeith

General Information

Dalkeith Country Park lies within a beautiful walled estate owned by the Duke of Buccleuch, accessible from the eastern end of Dalkeith High Street.

The Scotts of Buccleuch bought the estate in 1642, and is now one of four estates in Scotland owned by the Duke of Buccleuch and Queensberry KT. Although a working estate, the Duke of Buccleuch lives mainly at his residence at Bowhill, near Selkirk, in the Scottish Borders

Other features of the estate are St. Mary's Episcopal Church, by David Bryce and William Burn (1835), a fine stone-built conservatory, by William Burn (1832), stables by William Adam (1740) and the Montagu Bridge by Robert Adam (1792), which is regarded as a fine example of his architecture.

The estate comprises of over 850 acres of farmland and woodland and offers incredible views of many species of mammal and bird. A ranger service is available and provides guided walks and personalised photographic and wildlife watching tours. The park is easily accessed by road and its proximity to Edinburgh provides rail and airport links. Remnants of the *Forest of Caledon* in the '*Old Wood*' form a Site of Special Scientific Interest (SSSI).

Dalkeith

The Scottish Castles Association

Background

At the launch of the first Fife Castles guidebook at Fernie Castle, the Laird of Balgonie and Eddergoll, was trying to persuade his colleagues to form an association of castle owners. His efforts were fruitless, mainly through a lack of available time. I thought about it for a few days, and then wrote to the Laird offering administrative help.

From a mail shot of around 350 to what was believed to be occupied castles in February 1996, there were some 70 responses, not all of which were positive. Nevertheless there was a core of owners who wished to pursue the possibility of an organisation. Eventually an initial meeting was held at Culcreuch Castle in Stirlingshire, and attended by seven owners (John & Nancy Wright (Plane Tower), Gemma Howard (Wormistone), Tom Clarke (Lochhouse Tower), David Littlefair (Culcreuch Castle), Gerald Coulson (Kelly Castle), Raymond and Stuart Morris (Balgonie Castle) and Iain MacIver (Strathendry Castle).

For the next 18 months, membership grew gradually as, in parallel, the Association defined its constitution, aims and objectives etc., and also organised its first castle visit weekend, in Fife, coupled with its first AGM, at Balgonie Castle. Further visits were held in June (East Lothian) and September (Aberdeenshire), before a crucial "Way Forward" workshop at Culcreuch Castle.

As the organisation approaches its 10th anniversary in 2006, it is now well established and has many robust attributes: -

- There had been 35 visit events by the end of 2004, typically five per year (February, April, May, June and September) and in the main, to castles not open to the public
- A vibrant and comprehensive newsletter published twice per year
- Regular challenging conferences promoting quality advice and information, which has attracted leading dignitaries from the architectural world, and castle owners
- A technology strategy, which encompasses a web site (www.scottishcastles association.com), supported by an information centre, of which an image database (photographs, plans and conjectures) is the first element. Its objective is to have a record of every castle where there is still visible remains.

Currently it has 80% population. Access has been granted to Historic Scotland, the Royal Commission on the Ancient and Historical Monuments of Scotland and the Westphalian Castles Group, which is part of the German Castles Association.

- A developing educational programme with significant partners to produce a castles CD for every primary, secondary and tertiary learning establishment in Scotland.
- An increasing membership, which includes over 70 castle owners

The Association has been very fortunate to have had two excellent Presidents. Initially Nigel Tranter O.B.E led it up to his untimely death, and then currently Lord Steel of Aikwood.

The Association seeks to achieve its objectives by: –

- Improving the public's awareness of Scottish castles as a valuable inheritance and tangible reminder of its cultural heritage
- Attracting as wide a membership as possible, encompassing castle owners, keepers and carers; potential owners and restorers; architects, artists and craftsmen; academics, students, writers and historians; and enthusiastic members of the general public
- Providing a forum for interested individuals and organisations to discuss issues of common concern
- Taking an active role in ensuring that appropriate methods of conservation and restoration are used
- Encouraging the responsible

ownership, conservation and restoration of ruined structures, and other buildings at risk, in the belief that, in many cases, restoration offers the best means of ensuring their long-term survival
- Promoting the academic study of Scottish castles, of the circumstances which gave rise to their creation, and of all the people and activities associated with them
- Building up knowledge and skills databases for use by all members
- Providing advice on repair and restoration
- Bringing together potential restorers with appropriate properties for restoration
- Liaising with other bodies, including government departments, local authorities and other conservation organisations, in the pursuit of the above objectives
- Organising national and international meetings in the context of the above objectives

Membership

Membership is available to all, and enquiries should be directed to the
SCA Administrative Office
Balgonie Castle
By Markinch
Fife, Scotland
KY7 6HQ

Royal Commission on the Ancient and Historical Monuments of Scotland

Recording and promoting Scotland's built heritage

The Royal Commission on the Ancient and Historical Monuments of Scotland (RCAHMS) records, interprets and collects information relating to Scotland's buildings, archaeology and maritime sites, and promotes its use through educational and outreach activities.

Whether you are researching family or local history, or simply keen to know more about the built environment of Scotland, we can provide a wealth of historical information and visual material.

Our Resources:
- historic and modern photographs
- aerial photographs from the 1940s to the present day
- architects' plans and antiquarian drawings
- modern survey drawings of buildings and archaeological sites
- excavation records
- maps dating back to the mid-19th century
- over 200 family photograph albums
- historic sketches and engravings
- manuscript material
- reference books and periodicals

Visit our public search room:
open Monday to Friday 9:30am to 4:30pm
consult our collections and access our online facilities
staff are on hand to assist with your research

Search our website:
- search our databases free-of-charge, with text-search or map-search
- find out what information and collection items we hold for sites around Scotland
- view thousands of images online and download for personal research
- access latest news, user guides, online exhibitions, downloadable documents and dedicated pages for learners and the press
- purchase digital images, prints, photocopies and a range of publications

Contact:
RCAHMS, John Sinclair House, 16 Bernard Terrace, Edinburgh EH8 9NX
Tel: +44 (0)131 662 1456
Fax: +44 (0)131 662 1477
Email: nmrs@rcahms.gov.uk
Website: www.rcahms.gov.uk

Land Reform Act
- Access Rights

Everyone, whatever their age or ability, has access rights established by the Land Reform (Scotland) Act 2003, but you only have those rights if you exercise them responsibly.

You can exercise these rights over most land and inland water in Scotland, including mountains, moorland, woods and forests, grassland, margins of fields in which crops are growing, paths and tracks, rivers and lochs, the coast and most parks and open spaces. Access rights can be exercised at any time of the day or night.

You can exercise access rights for recreational purposes (such as pastimes, family and social activities, and more active pursuits like horse riding, cycling, wild camping and taking part in events), educational purposes (concerned with furthering a person's understanding of the natural and cultural heritage), some commercial purposes (where the activities are the same as those done by the general public) and for crossing over land or water.

Existing rights, including public rights of way and navigation, and existing rights on the foreshore, continue.

The main places where access rights do not apply are: -

- Houses and gardens, and non-residential buildings and associated land
- Land in which crops are growing
- Land next to a school and used by the school
- Sports or playing fields when these are in use and where the exercise of access rights would interfere with such use
- Land developed and in use for recreation and where the exercise of access rights would interfere with such use
- Golf courses (but you can cross a golf course provided you don't interfere with any games of golf)
- Places like airfields, railways, telecommunication sites, military bases and installations, working quarries and construction sites; and
- Visitor attractions or other places, which charge for entry.
- Local authorities can formally exempt land from access rights for short periods. Local authorities and some other public bodies can introduce bye-laws.

Access rights do not extend to: -

- Being on or crossing land for the purpose of doing anything, which is an offence, such as theft, breach of the peace, nuisance, poaching, allowing a dog to worry livestock, dropping litter, polluting water or disturbing certain wild birds, animals and plants
- Hunting, shooting or fishing
- Any form of motorised recreation or passage (except by people with a disability using a vehicle or vessel adapted for their use)
- Anyone responsible for a dog, which is not under proper control; or to
- Anyone taking away anything from the land for a commercial purpose.

Statutory access rights do not extend to some places or to some activities that the public have enjoyed on a customary basis, often over a long period of time. Such access is not affected by the Land Reform (Scotland) Act 2003 and will continue.